*"And We have not sent you
but as a mercy to the worlds."*

The Qur'an, Surah 21:107

The Prophet of Islam
MUHAMMAD ﷺ

A Biography & Pictorial Guide to His Teachings
Featuring the Moral Bases of Islamic Civilization

Sam Deeb and Steven Scholl

White Cloud Press
Ashland, Oregon

Published by White Cloud Press in collaboration
with Islamic Sciences and Research Academy Australia

This book is available in quantity at special discounts for your group or
organization. For further information on permissions or sales, please contact:
White Cloud, PO Box 3400, Ashland, Oregon, 97520
Phone: 541.488.6415
email: info@whitecloudpress.com
or visit: www.whitecloudpress.com

Library of Congress Cataloging-in-Publication Data
Deeb, Sam.
 The prophet of Islam : biography and pictorial guide / Dr. Sam Deeb &
Steven Scholl.
pages cm
Includes bibliographical references and index.
ISBN 978-1-935952-79-4 (pbk. : alk. paper)
1. Muhammad, Prophet, -632--Biography. I. Scholl, Steven, 1954- II. Title.
BP75.D34 2013
297.6'3--dc23
[B]

First edition, 2014

Disclaimer & Notes

When Muslims mention Muhammad's name, they express their respect and sincerity of belief by saying, "God's Mercy, Blessing, and Peace be upon him." In Arabic, it is written like this (ﷺ).

In this book, written primarily as an introduction to the life of Muhammad for non-Muslims, we have not added this phrase in Arabic, English, or in abbreviation. The authors intend no disrespect to Muslim tradition, but feel that as Muhammad is referred to on nearly every page of the book such an insertion would prove a distraction to readers.

• *The Pocket Guide* refers at times to God as "Allah." It is important to note that Allah is for Muslims the same God of Judaism and Christianity, its sister monotheist faiths. Jews and Christians share several Hebrew words for God (for example, "Yahweh" and "Elohim," and God in Aramaic, the language of Jesus, is "Elah" or "Alaha"). Allah is the equivalent Arabic term. For example, in Arabic translations of the New Testament, God is always translated as Allah. As we shall see in the book, Muhammad clearly acknowledged the truth of the prophets of the Jewish and Christian Bibles, and affirmed that Muslims,

Christians, and Jews are all "people of the Book"; that is, they share a common monotheistic faith tradition. Each faith has its unique religious teachings, but for Muhammad they are part of a great, single Abrahamic faith. In the Qur'an we read:

"Surely those who believe, and those who are Jews, and the Christians, and the Sabians—whoever believes in God and the Last Day and does good, they shall have their reward from their Lord. And there will be no fear for them, nor shall they grieve" (Surah 2:62).

• Transliteration of Arabic words into English will be done based on recognized scholarly consensus but without using special diacritical marks to indicate phonetic preciseness. Arabic words that have become recognized in English usage will follow Webster's spelling, for example, the cities of Mecca and Medina. When helpful, an exact transliteration and discussion of the full meaning of the original Arabic may be used to provide a clear picture of the historical events under discussion.

• The content of this pocket guide is taken from reliable sources according to the research made by the authors. A list of our sources is included in our bibliography. Readers may email their comments and any questions they may have about the book's contents to: pocketguide@whitecloudpress.com

My similarity in comparison with the other prophets before me is that of a man who has built a house completely and excellently, except for a place of one brick. When people see the house, they admire its beauty and say: How splendid the house will be if the missing brick is put in its place! So I am that brick, and I am the last of the prophets.

Muhammad
(peace be upon him)
(Narrated by Bukhari 4.734, 4.735)

IT IS A GREAT HONOR to be involved in this literary project, to write a concise account of the life and teachings of the Prophet Muhammad (peace be upon him), the man who enlightened the hearts of millions of people around the world and taught them the nature of faith and submission to the One God, the Lord of the world and all beings.

This project brought me closer to the life, sayings, and deeds of Muhammad. I love him and admire him. The more I came to know him and understand his teachings and way of life, the more motivated I was to present this material to the world in a simple and reliable way.

Muhammad: the man who devoted his life for a noble cause and described himself humbly as the final brick that completed a beautiful building, a symbol for all the prophets and messengers God has sent to guide humanity to the truth and protect them from going astray. This process began with Adam, the father of humanity, followed by the likes of Noah, Abraham, Moses, David, Solomon, Zachariah, John the Baptist, and Jesus (peace and blessing be upon them all).

Muhammad revered all true prophets and messengers

that came before him, and acknowledged Jesus with a special honor when he gave the good news that Jesus will return one day before the end of life on earth. He will fight evil, end conflicts, and unite all believers in God under his banner. Muhammad asked all Muslims to follow Jesus when he returns and beware of the false messiah.

This pictorial guide is written in an illustrative, easy reading style. It is especially written for non-Muslims, including those visiting Muslim countries and sites associated with Islamic history and Muslim faith.

The pocket guide is divided into color coded chapters that consist of bold titled paragraphs for easy reading and quick reference.

I am deeply indebted and profoundly grateful to Mr. Mohammed Dib Abdul Razzak, Mrs. Sylvana Mahmic, Mrs. Vicki Snowdon, Dr. Zachariah Mathews, Mr. Peter Gould, Mr. Cyrille Bouzy, Mr. Mehmet Ozalp, and all individuals who contributed to enhance the presentation of the text and its content.

Dr. Sam Deeb

I MET SAM DEEB at the Islamic Society of North America convention in Chicago in July 2011. We struck up a friendly conversation at the White Cloud Press exhibit, where I was sharing with my Muslim friends books on Islam published by White Cloud. Sam showed me an earlier version of the Pocket Guide, which I very much appreciated but also felt was not yet written in a style that would best reach non-Muslim readers. After a long conversation at the booth, we decided to explore a collaboration, where I would work with the original text and include new details that I thought would help readers with little or no familiarity with Islam.

I should make clear here at the start that I am not a Muslim. I have been deeply engaged in the study of Islam since 1978, when I began my academic study of religion. After receiving my Bachelor's degree in history of religion, I went on to do graduate studies at the Institute of Islamic Studies, McGill University, and lived for a year in Cairo to deepen my knowledge and understanding of the religion that began with the revelations to Muhammad. I continue my engagement with the Muslim world through friendships with Muslims and by leading small group tours of Americans eager to learn first-hand about Islam by traveling to Muslim majority countries.

Working on this book has been a special experience, and led me to an even deeper appreciation of the Prophet Muhammad, who is without doubt one of the most remarkable religious figures in human history. My hope is that readers of this little book will approach Muhammad with an open mind and open heart. He is not to be judged quickly and by strictly twenty-first century standards. He was very much a man of his time, but like all great figures of history, he also transcended his time through his vision, courage, and profound moral sensibilities.

Unfortunately, centuries of Jewish-Christian-Muslim competition (theological and political) has led to a tremendous amount of angry rhetoric around this man and between believers in the Abrahamic faiths. Each of the three faiths tends toward exclusivism, seeing their religion as either "the one true religion" or maintaining that "my faith is better than your faith." Yet against these strands of Jewish, Christian, and Muslim exclusivism, there are scriptural exhortations calling for believers to manifest kindness and love toward their neighbors who follow a different religion.

Two passages from the Qur'an make clear the difficult but fundamental commandment to combat the religious impulse toward exclusivism while respecting religious diversity:

"To everyone of you we have appointed a sacred law and a course to follow. For, had God so wished, He would have made you all one community. Rather, He wished to try you by means of what He had given you; who among you is of the best action. Compete therefore with one another as if in a race in the performance of good deeds. To God shall be your return, and He will inform you concerning the things in which you had differed" (Surah 5:48).

"Do not debate with the people of the Book save in the fairest manner . . . and say to them: we accept faith in that which was sent down to us [that is the Qur'an] and that which was sent down to you [that is the Torah and the Gospel]. Our God and your God is one" (Surah 29:46).

All of us involved in this book, Muslims and non-Muslims, sincerely hope that it will make a small contribution to understanding the religious pluralism that exists in the world and that this diversity of faith is something that will lead to peace, not war.

Steven Scholl

IACA-Dubai

FANAR
Qatar Islamic Cultural Center

ISRA
ISLAMIC SCIENCES &
RESEARCH ACADEMY
AUSTRALIA

Acknowledgements

Special thanks and gratitude to:

Al Medina Research and Studies Center
Medina - Saudi Arabia

Ministry of Awqaf (Endowments) and Islamic Affairs
Kuwait

Islamic Affairs and Charitable Activities Department
Dubai - UAE

Ministry of Awqaf, and Islamic Affairs, Jordan

Ahmed Al-Fateh Islamic Center, Bahrain

Malaysia Department of Islamic Development – JAKIM

Fanar, Islamic Cultural Center – Qatar

Islamic Sciences and Research Academy of Australia

For their kind support and cooperation

Table of
Contents

This is the word "Muhammad" in Arabic written in a formative style. It looks like the upper part of a mosque with a dome in the middle. Please note the dome is the letter "h" in the word "Muhammad." The lower part of the mosque is formed from the sentence "rasul-Allah" which means the "Messenger of God."

The hexagon is formed from the Arabic word "Muhammad" being written in a different style of Arabic calligraphy and repeated six times.

Courtesy of Plastic Artist Farid Al-Ali

In Arabic, the word "Muhammad" means the person who is highly, frequently, and repeatedly praised for his good deeds. Therefore, he is a praiseworthy person.

Chapter 1

Testimonials

Karen Armstrong
Author of *Muhammad a Prophet for Our Time*

"Muhammad literally sweated with the effort to bring peace to war-torn Arabia. His life was a tireless campaign against greed, injustice, and arrogance.

"If we are to avoid catastrophe, the Muslim and Western Worlds must learn not merely to tolerate but to appreciate one another. A good place to start is with the figure of Muhammad."

William Montgomery Watt
(1909–2006)—The Scottish historian and emeritus professor in Arabic and Islamic Studies at the University of Edinburgh. Author of *Muhammed: Prophet and Statesman*.

"His readiness to undergo persecutions for his beliefs, the high moral character of the men who believed in him and looked up to him as leader, and the greatness of his ultimate achievement—all argue his fundamental integrity. None of the great figures of history is so poorly appreciated in the West as Muhammad."

Deepak Chopra
Best selling author of *Muhammad: The Story of the Last Prophet*

"What drew me to this story [of the Muhammad] was my fascination with the way in which consciousness rises to the level of the divine. This phenomenon links Buddha, Jesus, and Muhammad. Higher consciousness is universal. It is held out as the ultimate goal of life on earth. Without guides who reached higher consciousness, the world would be bereft of its greatest visionaries—fatally bereft, in fact. Muhammad senses this aching gap in the world around him. He appeals to me most because he remade the world by going inward. That's the kind of achievement only available on the spiritual path. In light of what the Prophet achieved, he raises my hopes that all of us who lead everyday lives can be touched by the divine."

John Adair
Chair of Leadership Studies United Nations System Staff College in Turin and author of *The Leadership of Muhammad*.

"Leadership glimpsed more than once in the life of the Prophet Muhammad accords well with what we know to be the universal truth about the nature and practice of leadership."

Mahatma Gandhi
(1869 –1948)—The political and spiritual leader of the Indian independence movement.

"I wanted to know the best one who holds today undisputed sway over the hearts of millions of mankind. I became more than convinced that it was not the sword that won a place for Islam in those days in the scheme of life. It was the rigid simplicity, the utter self-effacement of the Prophet, the scrupulous regard for his pledges, his intense devotion to his friends and followers, his intrepidity, his fearlessness, and his absolute trust in God and in his own mission. When I closed the second volume (of the book about his life) I was sorry that there was not more for me to read about his great life."

Alphonse de Lamartine
(1790–1869)—A French poet, writer, and politician, author of *Histoire De La Turquie*

"Philosopher, orator, apostle, legislator, warrior, conqueror of ideas, restorer of rational dogmas, of a cult without images; the founder of twenty terrestrial empires and of one spiritual empire. That is Muhammad. As regards all standards by which human greatness may be measured, we may well ask, is there any man greater than him?"

William Durant
(1885–1981)—The American historian, philosopher and author of *The Story of Civilization*.

"His name, meaning, "highly praised," lent itself well to certain Biblical passages as predicting his advent. Muhammad was never known to write anything himself; he used an amanuensis. His apparent illiteracy did not prevent him from composing (i.e. conveying the Holy Qur'an which was revealed to him and regarded as) the most famous and eloquent book in the Arabic tongue, and from acquiring such understanding of the management of men as seldom comes to highly educated persons."

Johann Wolfgang Von Goethe
(1749–1832)—A great European poet, scientist, and philosopher.

"He is a prophet and not a poet and therefore his Qur'an is to be seen as Divine Law and not as a book of a human being made for education or entertainment."

Thomas Carlyle
(1795–1881)—The Scottish historian, philosopher and author of *Heroes and Hero Worship and the Heroic in History.*

"How one man single-handedly, could weld warring tribes and wandering Bedouins into a most powerful and civilized nation in less than two decades."

Leo Tolstoy
(1828–1910)—The famous Russian writer and novelist; author of *War and Peace.*

"There is no doubt that Prophet Muhammad is one of the greatest reformers who served the social framework profoundly. It suffices him that he led a whole nation to the enlightenment of truth and made it more inclined towards tranquility and peace, and prevented it from shedding blood and giving human sacrifices (though this was never proved against Arabs before Islam). He widely opened to his nation the gate to development and civilization. This is a great deed that only a strong man can do and a man like that deserves to be regarded with respect and admiration."

Chapter 2

His Character

Muhammad Attributes Portrait : *Documented character and attributes as seen by his companions.*
Produced by the Spanish calligrapher Nuria García Masip

Muhammad's Character

Unlike the founders of the great faith traditions prior to his time, the Prophet Muhammad is much more a recognizable historical figure. We have little historical records of the lives of Jesus and Buddha, and even less for Abraham and Moses. But Muhammad appears on the pages of history as a known figure, as his companions and family members recorded stories from his life for posterity.

What did he look like?

Muhammad was an Arab of noble lineage with a white complexion and a rosy tinge. He was a little taller than average and well built with broad shoulders. His belly never protruded out from his chest. He walked briskly and firmly.

Muhammad's companions described him as a handsome man with a prominent forehead, high tipped nose, long eyelashes, large black eyes with well-set teeth, and a pleasant smile. He had slightly curly hair and a thick beard.

His companions also indicated that Muhammad had a friendly, bright face that looked like a full moon. He did not laugh loudly; his laugh was mostly a smile that would show his teeth, which were a bit like hailstones. All felt his cheerfulness and open personality.

His nature

Muhammad was unfailingly cheerful, easy going by nature, and mild mannered. He had a refined way about of speaking, never resorting to vulgar speech or obscenities. He did not find fault with others nor did he overly praise his companions.

The way he spoke

Muhammad chose his words carefully, he always said what he meant, was direct and to the point. He spoke in a beautiful manner with no excess but also without being too short in conveying his ideas and intents. When he emphasized a point, he used to repeat it three times with a gesture. He once told his companions:

"I am a guarantor for a house at outskirts of Paradise for those who quit arguing even if they were right; and I am a guarantor for a house in the middle of Paradise for those who quit lying even if they were kidding; and I am a guarantor for a house in the highest part of Paradise for those who behave with good manners." (From *Sahih Abu Dawud*)

His passions

Muhammad kept his feelings under firm control. When annoyed, he would turn aside or keep silent. When someone committed an act that violates God's law, he used to show serious anger and took a firm stand for the way of righteousness. No one would stand against his anger in matters of the Lord's truth being opposed, he would stand fast in protecting the truth until he had convinced another of the rightness of God's truth as revealed in the Qur'an. Muhammad never got angry for his own sake.

His interactions with people

Muhammad was always the first to greet others and would not withdraw his hand from a handshake until the other man withdrew his. He was gentle by nature and all were attracted to this aspect of his personality. When he met someone, he looked at them directly, fully. If someone called to him, he didn't just turn his face but gave attention with his whole body. He was deeply present to whomever he was with in each moment.

When he visited a group, he would sit in the nearest available spot. He ordered his companions to follow his practice. He gave those seated near him his full attention in such a way that no one felt that others had been given precedence over any one else. He didn't reserve fixed places among the people to be seated. He was fair with his companions and all people. For Muhammad, what distinguished a man or woman were their virtues and their devotion to God.

His style of living

Everything the Prophet Muhammad did was in moderation. He never criticized the food or drink that was prepared for him, nor did he overly praise it. When at home, he would divide his time into three parts: one for God, one for his family, and one for himself. He always joined in household work and would at times mend his own clothes, repair his shoes, and sweep the floor.

He dressed well but modestly and enjoyed the beautiful fragrance of perfume oils on the body.

After dawn prayers, he would remain sitting in the mosque reciting the Holy Qur'an and praises of God until the sun rose. After midnight, he would get up for the night prayers, which he never missed.

He declared unlawful for himself and his family anything of the alms (*zakat*) given by Muslims for the welfare of those in need. He was so particular about this that he would not appoint any member of his family as a collector of alms for the community.

His house was a modest building, some would even say it was a simple hut, with walls of unbaked clay and a thatched roof of palm leaves covered by camel skin.

Muhammad said: "What have I to do with worldly things? My connection with the world is like that of a traveler resting for a while underneath the shade of a tree and then moving on."

When he died, Muhammad did not leave a cent or any property except his white mule and a piece of land that he had dedicated for the good of the community of Muslims.

Prophet Muhammad's Mosque as described and imagined

Prophet Muhammad's house as described and imagined

Chapter 3

Biography

Personal Details

Name	**Muhammad**
Father	Abdu'llah, son of Abdu'l-Muttalib
Clan and Tribe	He was from the Banu Hashim family, a respected family that was part of the Quraysh, the ruling tribe of Mecca.
Date of Birth	22 April 570 CE [1]
Place of Birth	City of Mecca in the Arabian Peninsula
Date of Death	6 June 632 CE. He was 63 years old when he passed away.
Place of Death & Burial	City of Medina, approximately 450 km north of Mecca.

Childhood & Adolescence

Birth - 2 years old	Muhammad had no brothers or sisters. His father passed away before he was born. His mother, Amina, sent him out of Mecca to be breastfed by a wet nurse, named Halima. This was a custom to instill Bedouin culture among the Arab people.
2-6 years old	He lived with his mother until she passed away in the year 576 CE.
6-8 years old	He lived with his grandfather, Abdu'l-Muttalib, until his grandfather's death in 578 CE.
8-25 years old	He lived with his paternal uncle, Abu-Talib, who had ten children.

Education

In the Qur'an, Muhammad is referred to in Arabic as *an-nabiyy al-ummiyy*, a term often understood and translated as "illiterate" or "unlettered prophet."

Many scholars, both Muslim and non-Muslim, suggest that the phrase "unlettered prophet" is used in the Qur'an in the context of discussions about how Jews and Christians were "people of the Book"—that is, were monotheists who had divine guidance through prophets and scriptures.

In contrast, Muhammad came to a people that until his time did not have such divine guidance through scripture. The Arab tribes were living in ignorance and needed prophetic wisdom, which was now being given to them through the revelations coming to Muhammad. In other words, the term may mean that he was a prophet to a people without scripture, who were themselves unlettered in monotheistic faith.

What we do know is that Muhammad did not write down the Qur'an. The holy book of Islam is, as it's name declares, "a recitation," the book was received by Muhammad through the angel Gabriel, and Muhammad recited what the angel conveyed to him word for word (see next the chapter on "Muhammad and Prophecy").

Working Life

Childhood – mid-twenties: Muhammad worked as a shepherd for some time. In addition, he worked in trading with his uncle, Abu-Talib. Muhammad was twelve-years old when he went on his first trading trip to Syria with his uncle.

Mid-twenties – 40 years old: Muhammad worked as a trader for a wealthy woman, Khadijah, buying commodities from one area and selling them in another. Muhammad was known in his community as a successful and honest tradesman. He was famous for his fidelity, integrity, and trustworthiness, and became known by the title of *As-Sadiqu'l-Ameen*, which means "the truthful and the trustworthy."

40-63 years old: When he was forty, in the year 610 CE, Muhammad received the first divine relations and dedicated his life to conveying God's message to all people. He taught the oneness of God and delivered faithfully God's book, The Qur'an.

Marital Status

Married to one wife for twenty-five years: Khadijah was a respected woman in her community. She was a widow who successfully ran a trading enterprise. Her life story puts to the test many prejudices about the status of women in Islam. Here we see a woman who ran her own business and controlled her economic affairs centuries before women in the Western world had such options. Muhammad worked for her for two years before she proposed marriage to him through a third party. She found him a very loyal, transparent, and ethical person.

Successful marriage: Although Khadijah was fifteen years older than Muhammad, both of them came from a similar social class. Their age difference was no obstacle to the establishment of a successful marriage, which was founded on love, affection, and great respect for each other. Their marriage lasted for twenty-five years until Khadijah died in the year 619 CE at the age of sixty-five. Muhammad remarried after Khadijah's death.

> **Muhammad loved Khadijah and was loyal to her**
>
> On several occasions he described her as the best woman of her time, alike to Mary, the mother of Jesus who was the best woman of her time.

A father of six children and a family man:

Muhammad and Khadijah lived in harmony and peace. They had four daughters (Zaynab, Ruqayyah, Umm Khulthum, and Fatimah) and two sons (Al-Qassim, who died when he was three, and Abdullah, who died at age four). He was a devoted husband and father who spent time with his family, helped his wife in house matters, sewed his own clothes, and looked after his children.

Photo taken from Baqee Cemetery which is next to the Prophet Muhammad Mosque in Medina. Some of Muhammad's companions, relatives, wives, and children are buried in this cemetery.

Al-Ma'ala cemetery in Mecca where Khadijah is buried

Mission Accomplished in 23 Years

610 CE
Divine revelation begins:

In the year 610 CE, Muhammad received the first revelations from the Angel Gabriel of words that would come to be known as The Qur'an. He was called to convey God's words to humanity. This was to be a mission that ran counter to the cultural and economic powers of his time, and required  of Muhammad strong belief, dedication, commitment, and an unswerving allegiance to God. (See "Prophecy" chapter for more details on the revelation of God's message to Muhammad.)

610- 612 CE
The first believers:

Muhammad invited his inner circle of friends to accept Islam, and then gradually expanded the number of new

 Muslims. In the first three years of his mission, around 130 people accepted Islam, a mix of rich and poor. This became the strong core of believers, who began to spread the message of Islam among the people of Mecca and those who came to

Mecca for trading and pilgrimage to the Kaaba with its 360 idols.

613- 615 CE
Muhammad's message resisted:
Muhammad and his followers began speaking openly about Islam. Though Muhammad was respected among the Quraysh leaders of Mecca, they saw the teachings of Islam as a threat to their economic monopoly and power over the pagan populace.

Muhammad tempted and threatened: The Meccan ruling elite tried to dissuade Muhammad from calling people to Islam by tempting and threatening him. At the same time, they tried to prevent people from listening to him. They showed increased hostility toward new Muslim and they persecuted and tortured poor and weak Muslims. The Quraysh elite recognized that their position was threatened by Muhammad's revelations that critiqued the religious, moral, and economic corruption of the times.

Muhammad supported by his followers; sends some of them to Abyssinia: Each early convert risked their reputation and possibly their livelihood and their lives by accepting Islam. This led to a great bond between Muhammad and his followers. Muhammad would meet with these early converts at Al-Arqam's House. Al-Arqam was a young, wealthy, and influential member of the Quraysh clan, an early convert and important supporter of Muhammad.

His home became like a small college or seminary for study and discussion of the new religion. In this setting, Muhammad taught his followers values and morals, and it was here that the new forms of Islamic prayer began to take form.

Muhammad saw the suffering that some of his followers endured and he advised them to seek refuge in Abyssinia across the Red Sea, describing it as a land ruled by a just Christian king. Muhammad may also have been thinking of some kind of monotheistic alliance between Christian Abyssinia and the new Muslim movement against the pagan forces in Arabia.

At this time, two strong and respected Meccan leaders converted to Islam: Umar bin Al-Khattab and Hamza bin Abdu'l-Muttalib (the latter was Muhammad's uncle). This was an important turning point for Muslims, who took heart that such strong Arab leaders had joined their cause. Hamza became a strong supporter and protector of Muhammad. He confronted Muhammad's most dangerous adversary, Abu Jahl, who had taken to hurling abuse and insults at Muhammad when the Prophet preached at the Kaaba.

Umar had been a fierce opponent of Muhammad's. When he heard that his sister and her husband had become Muslims, he became enraged and struck his sister so hard that she bled. He was immediately shamed by this outburst and agreed to listen to verses of the Qur'an. He was so moved that he went directly to Muhammad to express his faith as a Muslim. Umar became the second caliph to lead the Muslims after Muhammad's death.

Muhammad boycotted: Meccan leaders boycotted Muhammad and his followers, imposing a social and economic blockade on them that lasted three years. During this time, Muhammad and these first converts suffered greatly. This period put the early Muslims to a test of faith that called for patience and commitment to the truth.

619- 620 CE

A sorrowful year: The Meccan chiefs cancelled the boycott on Muslims as they came to see it caused more harm than good to their designs. But this relief was short-lived as Muhammad lost two of his most important supports—his beloved wife Khadijah and his uncle and protector Abu-Talib both died.

Muhammad realized that he needed a more secure base from which to proceed with his mission as God's Messenger. He first went to the nearby city of Ta'if, located in the mountains southeast of Mecca, but was met with hostility.[4] He preached to over twenty Arab tribes, inviting them to Islam, but did not receive support in that direction either.

620- 622 CE

A glimpse of hope to the north: About 450 km north of Mecca, the oasis settlement of Yathrib was an important agricultural center. The oasis was about twenty square miles and was settled by eleven clans. The people of Yathrib were a mix of Arabs and Jews. It appears that in earlier times the Jewish tribes had been predominant at the oasis, but over time

Arab tribes came to outnumber the Jews. In Muhammad's time there were eight Arab and three Jewish clans. Also, Jews and Arabs intermarried so that the main cultural patterns were by this time predominantly Arab but the religious culture of Jewish monotheism was also strong in this area. In the oasis, where clans lived in close proximity, disputes were inevitable and frequent.

Conflicts between the various clans had escalated as there was no means of resolving disputes other than the Bedouin traditions of blood-feud. The people of Yahtrib were drawn to the charismatic figure of Muhammad, who was also an impartial outsider, and they sought him out to come north to act as judge and arbiter.

In the midst of the sorrow and despair Muhammad experienced with the loss of Khadijah and Abu-Talib, he met with six men from Yathrib. These men from the north represented six important clans of Yathrib. They had come to Mecca during the pilgrimage season to confirm their belief in the Quranic message and in Muhammad's role as Prophet of God. They returned to Yathrib with the intention of inviting more people from their oasis town to become Muslims. They agreed to return to Mecca the following year to meet again during the pilgrimage season.

New Muslims pledge allegiance to Muhammad: The same group returned in 621 CE with six more people representing more clans.[5] They all pledged their allegiance to Muhammad, accepting him as the Messenger of God, and promising to uphold Quranic values.

Aqaba or Al-Bay'aa "Pledge" Mosque

The group returned to Yathrib and invited their tribal leaders and all the people to accept Islam. The following year a delegation from Yathrib returned to Mecca, this time with more than 70 men and two women. All made a similar pledge to Muhammad. The fortunes of Muhammad and Islam were beginning to turn.

622 CE

Chiefs of Mecca plot to kill Muhammad, migration to Yathrib begins: The situation of Muhammad and the Muslims in Mecca was deteriorating. The Meccan leaders escalated their attacks on Muslims, and Muhammad was directly threatened with execution. Muhammad instructed his followers to quietly depart Mecca for Yathrib. Once the Quraysh realized what was happening, they attempted to kill Muhammad, but with his cousin Ali serving as a decoy and his trusted friend Abu-Bakr as his traveling companion, Muhammad fled Mecca and joined his companions in Yathrib. The migration (*hijra*) is the most important turning point in Muhammad's ministry and it is from this date that the Muslim calendar begins as Year One.

623-624 CE

Muhammad chosen as the ruler of Medina: Muhammad was greeted by the leaders and people of Yathrib as he approaches the oasis. He was acclaimed as the arbiter and ruler of the oasis, which now became known as the City of the Prophet, *Medinat an-nabi*. Now is known simply as Medina, the second most holy site for Muslims, where the Mosque of the Prophet and his tomb are located.

Muhammad's call for peace and unity in Medina: After the migration of the Meccan Muslims, Medina no longer became so rigidly divided along clan lines. Old divisions gave way to a new sense of solidarity as the majority of people converted to Islam. But there were still Jews and other Arabs in Medina who did not become Muslims. In his first public address to the people of Medina, Muhammad delivered a powerful speech that promoted harmony and social cohesion.

He said: "O People, seek and spread peace and offer food to each other, look after your kinship and pray to God at night while others are sleeping so you gain God's pleasure and enter his paradise."

Muhammad linked these acts to God's pleasure in order to motivate people to love each other and live in peace and harmony in a multicultural society.

Muhammad forms the first constitution and charter of human rights and liberties: In Medina, the various factions—Jews, Arab pagans, and Arab Muslims—all accepted Muhammad as their leader and mediator of disputes. To bring a greater sense of peace and justice to the troubled oasis of Medina, Muhammad drafted the Constitution of Medina, a remarkable document that established a charter of human rights and liberties for a plural society.

The constitution guaranteed the freedom of conscience and worship for Muslims, Jews, and Christians as well as Arabs who did not accept Islam. Furthermore, the constitution protected the safety and security of all citizens of Medina and required all parties who signed the charter to be part of the defense of Medina in the event of attack.

624 CE

The Battle of Badr: When the Meccan Muslims were forced to migrate to Medina due to persecution from the Quraysh clan, many of them were forced to abandon their homes and their wealth was taken. The chiefs of Mecca used this confiscated money in trade and business. Muslims knew about a trade caravan due to pass close to Medina belonging to the Meccan chiefs and led by their most fierce enemy Abu-Sufyan.

Location of Battle of Badr

Muhammad called on the Muslims to take the caravan in return for their wealth that had been stolen in Mecca. A force of only 313 Muslims took up the mission. Meccan intelligence advised Abu-Sufyan to change the caravan route. In addition, Mecca sent an army of 950 soldiers to fight the Muslim force. The Muslims were not a trained force and were far less equipped than the Meccan army. They were, however, determined and inspired by their faith.

It was not just a surprising victory but a turning point. Many important Meccan leaders were killed in this battle and for the first time the Meccan elite appeared vulnerable while the Muslims were clearly ascendant.

625 CE

Meccan chiefs attack Muhammad and his followers in the Battle of Uhud: In retaliation for their loss in the battle of Badr and their fear of losing their preeminence in Arabia, the Meccan chiefs with some allies sent an army of 3,000 soliders to attack Muslims on the hill known as Uhud just north of Medina.

The Muslims were again outnumbered but this time the results were not in their favor. They took many casualties, including Muhammad's beloved uncle Hamza. But the Meccans did not prevail either. Their goal was to destroy the Muslims and kill Muhammad. Though wounded, Muhammad lived and, again, the Meccans were hit hard and lost many warriors. In military terms, the battle of Uhud was a draw, but for some Muslims, following on the miracle at Badr, this was a disheartening moment.

626 CE

Meccans and other tribes attack Muhammad and his followers at the Battle of the Trench: With Muhammad surviving the Battle of Uhud, the Meccan chiefs realized that his leadership of the Muslims was a threat to their control of Arabia. The Meccan leadership raised a large assault force of 10,000 men from Arab and Jewish tribes with the goal to conquer Medina and kill Muhammad. Muhammad consulted with his top advisors. The Persian convert, Salman, proposed the digging of a trench on the northern access of Medina. The trench was nearly 5.5 km in length and 4.6 meters wide.

The trench prevented the Meccans from overrunning Medina and a month-long stalemate ensued. Then the weather grew worse with cold and strong storms, and the Meccan troops abandoned their assault and retreated back to Mecca. Their massive attempt to break Muhammad's power had failed.

627 CE

The Treaty of Hudaybiya, a 10-year truce: One year after the Battle of the Trench, Muhammad decided to make the pilgrimage to the Ka'bah at Mecca. Muhammad and 1,400 Muslims from Medina set out for Mecca to the surprise of the Meccan leaders.

Visiting Mecca for the purpose of worship was a religious right that the Meccans provided for all the people of Arabia. The Meccans sent out a delegation to meet with Muhammad and the parties settled on a truce to last ten years. Part of the truce was that Muhammad and his 1400 followers would return to Medina but would be allowed to return for pilgrimage in the following year.

10-Year Truce

The truce had many stipulations that some Muslims felt were unfair and gave too much to the pagan Meccans. But on the whole the treaty provided Muhammad and his followers with a firm base for further expansion of Islam throughout the Arabian Peninsula.

628- 629 CE

Expanding the House of Islam: The truce granted Muhammad the right to send out Muslim teachers to tribes and clans without being stopped or intercepted by Meccan warriors.

Muhammad sent delegations to Arab tribes and wrote letters to the rulers and kings of neighboring countries. The rulers of Persia, Egypt, and Byzantium were informed of the rise of Islam in Arabia. More and more people found the Message of the Qur'an convincing and converted to Islam. This expansion of Islam to the north of Mecca blocked trade routes and further weakened the position of the Meccan leadership.

630 CE

The peaceful takeover of Mecca: Less than two years after its signing, the truce was broken from the Meccan side when Meccan allies killed twenty Muslims. In response to this act of hostility, Muhammad marched with 10,000 men to secure Mecca as the spiritual center of the new faith. But this was not a traditional Arab conflict.

Muhammad asked his soldiers not to fight anyone unless they were attacked.[7]

The Meccan leaders were not prepared to fight an army this large. They also knew full well that the tide was turning against them. When Muhammad and his army reached Mecca, the Prophet addressed the entire population. He confirmed the oneness of God, acknowledged that victory comes from Him, and reminded the people of Mecca that all of them descended from Adam and that Adam was created from dust.

He asked the people of Mecca, "What do you expect me to do with you?" They replied, "We hope for the best. After all, you have been a gracious brother and a kind cousin."

Exemplar of forgiveness: Despite the hardship caused by the Meccan people during the previous twenty-one years, Muhammad responded with mercy and compassion: "Have no fear today, depart to your homes, you are free."

This forgiveness of enemies caused many Meccan leaders to have a change of heart, and they threw in their support by converting to Islam. In the end, the city fell with few casualties on either side while Muhammad preached peace and reconciliation.

It was becoming clear to all of Arabia, and especially the Meccans, that Muhammad's leadership and the values of the Qur'an provided greater security than Quraysh rule; there was rising hope for a better future. The pettiness, selfishness, and greed that motivated the Meccan aristocracy was no match for the new society Muhammad envisioned and was in the process of creating.

Fairness, social justice, equality, and greater rights for women and the poor attracted the support of the majority of Arabs. Muhammad, for so long attacked and despised in his native Mecca, was now triumphant, and his faith was ready to change the course of history.

630 - 631 CE

Arab tribes embrace Islam: After the peaceful takeover of Mecca, delegations from all over Arabia came to learn about Islam. Except for the Hawasen tribe, who fought on but eventually lost at the Battle of Hunayn, most Arab tribes embraced Islam. Muhammad sent many of his top companions to the various provinces in Arabia to teach the people the Qur'an and the teachings and prayers of Islam.

While in Mecca, Muhammad purified the Sacred Mosque by removing all idols from the Ka'bah.

632 CE

Muhammad's farewell address: Muhammad's mission was accomplished and his life was nearing its end. In 632 CE Muhammad performed pilgrimage to the Ka'bah and gave his final sermon to more than 100,000 people.

His sermon reminded people of the basic elements of faith, belief in one God, the sanctity of life and property, the equality of all races, rules of justice, women's rights and obligations, and moral precepts. Here is a brief excerpt from the final sermon:

All mankind is from Adam and Eve. An Arab has no superiority over a non-Arab, nor does a non-Arab have any superiority over an Arab; white has no superiority over black, nor does a black have any superiority over white; except by piety and good action. Learn that every Muslim is a brother to every Muslim and that the Muslims constitute one brotherhood . . . Remember, one day you will appear before God and answer for your deeds. So beware, do not stray from the path of righteousness after I am gone.

The death of Muhammad:

The Prophet Muhammad, peace be upon him, passed away in his home in Medina in the year 632 CE, leaving only a few possessions. He did not leave behind money or wealth; rather, he provided all people, Muslim and non-Muslims, with a legacy of faith in God's mercy and light that is still illuminating the hearts of millions of people around the globe.

Among the known prophets of God, Muhammad is the only prophet whose burial place is precisely identified. Muhammad was buried at his house, which is attached to the Al-Nabawi mosque in Medina.

This photo shows the side of the mosque where people can enter to see the tomb of Prophet Muhammad, as well as his house, which is currently surrounded by a metal fence.

Walking to the tomb of the Prophet

إِنَّ الَّذِينَ يَغُضُّونَ أَصْوَاتَهُمْ عِنْدَ رَسُولِ اللَّهِ أُولَئِكَ الَّذِينَ امْتَحَنَ اللَّهُ قُلُوبَهُمْ لِلتَّقْوَى لَهُمْ مَغْفِرَةٌ وَأَجْرٌ عَظِيمٌ

The tomb of Prophet Muhammad at the Nabawi Mosque in Medina (first on the left).

Next to it are the tombs of the first Caliph (successor) and ruler of the Islamic state Abu Bakr Al Siddiq, and the second Caliph, Omar Bin Al-Khattab.

The Prophet's Mosque (Al-Masjid Al-Nabawi Al-Sharif)
Photograph courtesy of Noushad Ali

Aerial view of Mecca, Saudi Arabia.
Showing the Sacred Mosque (Al-Masjid Al-Haram).
Courtesy of Suzan Eskandar

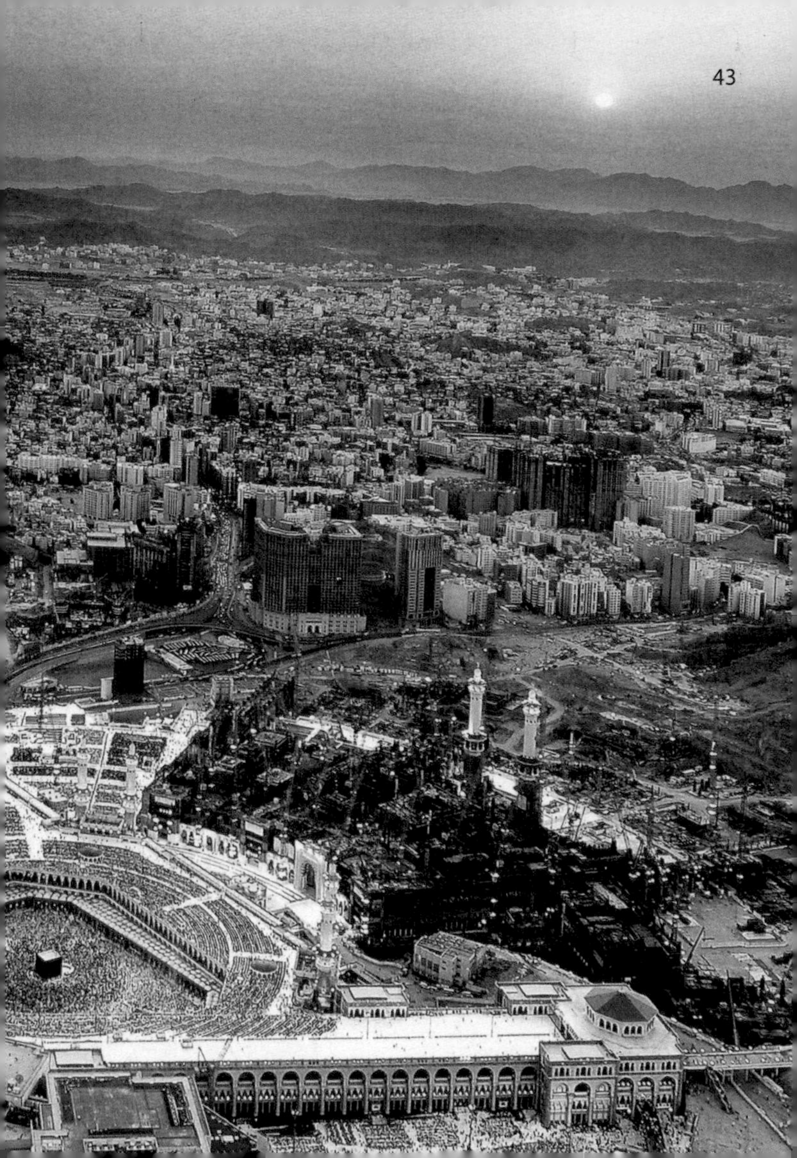

The Sacred Mosque (Al-Masjid Al-Haram) in Mecca, Saudi Arabia. This is the holiest Mosque in Islam. The black building is the Ka'bah. Muslims believe God Commanded Prophet Abraham to establish the Ka'bah to glorify and worship Him (the one God). When Muslims pray to God, they direct their faces (from all over the world) toward the Ka'bah.

NOTES

1. According to some narrations and calculations Muhammad was born in the year 571 CE.

2. Some narrations state that the marriage of Muhammad and Khadijah lasted for 24 years and several months.

3. There is one and only one Qur'an which is revealed to Muhammad in original Arabic. However, there are many translations for the meanings of the verses in the Holy Qur'an to different languages such as English, French, Chinese, etc. The quoted verses in this pocket guide from the Holy Qur'an are presented in simple English based on the English translation mentioned in the cited references.

4. Muhammad was attacked in Tai'f and experienced the worst treatment there. When he left Taif he was very disappointed. According to some narrations, he called God with a wonderful supplication (see next page).

5. Aqaba or Al-Bay'aa Mosque (Pledge Mosque): established by the Abbasside Caliph Abu Jaafar Al Manssour on the same place that is believed the new Muslims from Medina pledged commitment to Prophet Muhammad as they embraced Islam.

6. A small Muslim community stayed in Mecca and were not able to migrate to Yathrib (Medina).

7. The Islamic calendar starts from the date Muhammad migrated from Mecca to Medina (circ. September 13, 622 CE. The peaceful taking over of Mecca was circ. January 8, 630 CE).

Muhammad's Supplication To God

O my Lord, it is to You that I bring my weakness, helplessness & humiliation.

O The Most Merciful of the merciful ones, You are the Sustainer of those who are deemed weak and You are my Sustainer.

On whom (but You) shall I rely? On somebody distant who regards me with displeasure or on a foe to whom I have surrendered?

So long as You are not displeased with me, then I have no cause for sadness.

I take refuge in your light by which the darkness is illuminated and in which both this world and the next are set aright.

The well-being which You bestow upon me is too all-encompassing for You to pour out Your anger or displeasure upon me.

To You I shall continue to turn until I have won Your favor.

Chapter 4

Prophecy

Arabic calligraphy produced by the Japanese Calligrapher Nobuko Sagawa.

"And We have not sent you but to all people as a bearer of glad tidings and as a warner."

Surah 34:28

Mount of Noor Mecca

Muhammad & Prophecy

Muhammad didn't know that he would be a Prophet: Muhammad led an ethical and ordinary life. He was known for his fidelity, integrity, and trustworthiness. He never worshipped idols even though idol worship was common in a polytheistic society.

He always believed that the whole universe must have been created and controlled by one God. He used to worship God by retreating to a cave on a mountain four km east of Mecca.

The cave is known as Hira cave, and can be found at *Jabal al-Nur* (the mountain of light). Muhammad received the first revelation from God when he was meditating in this cave.

It wasn't illusion and it wasn't a dream:
In approximately 610 CE, in the month of Ramadan at the Hira Cave, the Archangel Gabriel appeared to Muhammad for the first time and commanded him to "Recite." Muhammad was frightened.

Recite !

Hira Cave

Muhammad told Gabriel, "I am not a reciter." Then Gabriel repeated his word "recite" again and again; then he pronounced the following verses from God:

> *Recite in the name of your Lord who created*
> *From and embryo created the human*
> *Recite your Lord is all-giving, who taught by the pen*
> *Taught the human what he did not know before.*
> Surah 96:1-5

Archangel Gabriel disappeared after this short meeting.

Muhammad was terrified: He ran back to his home. He was trembling. He told his wife Khadijah what had happened to him and asked her to cover him. She told him that God would not let him down or allow devils to touch him as he kept good relations with his relatives, helped the poor, and liked doing charity.

This is the word Muhammad in Arabic designed by Artist Abdul Majid Al Noerat. It simulates the climb of Muhammad on the mount of Nur (light), and his drive to learn about the One God, the Creator and Lord of all beings.

A divine revelation or satanic whisperings? Muhammad was afraid that he was possessed by evil. He went with his wife Khadijah to tell the whole story to Waraqa Bin Nawfal, a relative of Khadijah who was a Christian and knowledgeable in the Bible. Waraqa predicted that Muhammad would be a Prophet and assured him that what he experienced was a divine revelation similar to what Moses, the Prophet of the Jews, received. Waraqa wished to support Muhammad but he was very old at that time. He told Muhammad that he would be driven out of Mecca by his own people and would be treated with hostility.

You are God's Messenger: Muhammad needed a few days to settle down and didn't return to the mountain. After some time Archangel Gabriel came back to him and informed him that he would be a messenger of God (Allah the Glorified and Exalted) in order to convey His Divine Message to all people. Gabriel recited the following verses from God:

> *O you cloaked [enveloped in your garments]; arise and warn; and glorify your Lord; and purify your clothing; and keep away from bad deeds and don't consider your fulfillment of these orders as a favor to God or people; and be patient for the sake of your Lord.*
> Surah 74:1-7

Gabriel continued to come to Muhammad over a period of 23 years. During this period, God's Message to humankind (the Holy Qur'an) was revealed.

Muhammad conveyed Gods' Message to all people: Muhammad acted according to the revelation he received as from the year 610 CE. He invited the people in Arabia and outside Arabia to believe in one God (Allah) and obey His commandments, as they are set for the well-being of humanity.

What is the "Message" about? The Message of Islam is based on *aqidah*, i.e. a declaration of faith in One God and shariah, which means God's Law, the system and regulations that govern people's day to day transactions, activities and practices.

Faith and Law

Shariah is divided into three main branches: (1) Worship, such as daily prayers, fasting, supplications, giving *zakat* (alms), etc.; (2) Morals, such as right actions, etiquettes and values (honesty, sincerity, fidelity, love, cooperation, etc.); and (3) Life transactions and dealings with others, such as rules of justice, people's rights, commerce and business ethics, inheritance, etc.

Note: After receiving the divine revelation, Muhammad focused on teaching people monotheism (*aqidah*) for thirteen years. After migration to Medina, there was more focus on explaining and implementing Shariah.

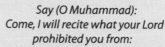

God's Commandments

Say (O Muhammad):
Come, I will recite what your Lord
prohibited you from:

(1) Don't join any partners as equal with Him;

(2) And be good to your parents;

(3) And don't kill your children on a plea of want, We provide sustenance for you and for them;

(4) And don't approach or get close to doing shameful deeds openly or secretly [e.g. adultery and deeds of corruption];

(5) And don't kill any soul which God made sacred except by way of justice and law. This is what He commands you, thus you may learn wisdom;

(6) And don't touch the orphans' wealth or property, except to improve it, until he or she reaches maturity;

(7) And give measure and

(8) weight with (full) justice [when buying and selling and when doing financial and non financial transactions], We place no burdens on any one but that which he or she can bear;

(9) And whenever you speak (or bear witness) speak justly even if a near relative is concerned;

(10) And fulfill the Covenant of God.

This is what He commands you that you may remember.

Surah 6:151-2

A practical introduction of Muhammad's teachings in Abyssinia: Ja'far bin Abi-Talib was among eighty Muslims who fled for protection in the land of Abyssinia (currently Ethiopia in Africa). Speaking to the King of Abyssinia on behalf of the Muslims who sought asylum there, Ja'far said:

"O King, we were once people living in ignorance worshiping idols, eating carrion, committing acts of abomination, neglecting our kith and kin, treating our neighbors badly, and allowing the strong among us to oppress the weak. This is how we lived until God sent us a messenger from among ourselves, a man whose origin, honesty, integrity, and chastity were well known to us.

He called upon us to worship God alone and leave away the stones and idols which we worshipped as our forefathers had done. He instructed us to be truthful in our words, to fulfill our promises and to respect our obligations to our blood relations, and he forbade us from committing abominations.

So we trusted and believed him and followed the message he received from God. However, our people denounced us, tortured us, and did everything in their capacity to turn us away from our religion. When they continued to oppress us, we came to your land choosing you above all others in order to get protection and be treated with impartiality."

A Christian King acknowledged Muhammad's religion:
After Ja'far delivered his talk, the King of Abyssinia (who was a religious and God-fearing person) asked Ja'far to recite some verses from the Book revealed to Muhammad.

Ja'far recited a portion from the surah Maryam,[1] the Mother of Jesus. He continued reciting until the King wept and his beard was moist with tears.

Negash, Mosque Tigray, Ethiopia

The King then said:

"The message brought by Muhammad and that which was brought by Jesus are from a single source."

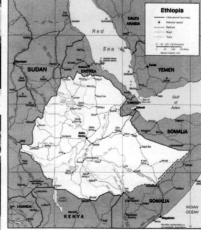

The Message of Islam

Islam in simple words: "Islam" means submission and devotion to One God. It is a religion of monotheism where the adherent to Islam believes that God is one and incomparable. He has no partners or sons. He begets not nor was he begotten (neither gives birth nor was born). He created the whole universe

Courtesy of Abdul Aziz Al Rashidi

and all beings. No one shares with Him His Divinity and no one has the right to be worshiped or prayed to but Him alone.

What is the name of God? In Arabic God's name is *Allah*. God has many attributes and adjectives. In Islam there are ninety- nine acknowledged "beautiful names" and attributes for Allah. For example God is "The Most Merciful" and "All-Knowing." No one can be more merciful than God and no one can be more knowledgeable than Allah.

English	Arabic	Hebrew	Aramaic
God	Elah	Eloha	Elaha

He is Allah besides Whom there is no God: The Knower of the unseen and the seen; He is the Beneficent, the Merciful.

He is Allah, besides Whom there is no God; the King, the Holy, the Author of Peace, the Granter of Security, Guardian over all, the Mighty, the Supreme, the Possessor of greatness. Glory be to Allah from that which they set up [with Him]!

He is Allah; the Creator, the Maker, the Fashioner: His are the most beautiful names. Whatever is in the heavens and the earth declares His glory; and He is the Mighty, the Wise.

Surah 59:22-24

Muhammad and Islam: When a man asked Muhammad to explain Islam in simple words so that he should not seek any further clarification from anyone else, Muhammad concisely said:

"Say, 'I believe in Allah [the one God] and then be straight.'"

Embracing the Islamic faith requires following a balanced way of life without diversion to extremism in actions, sayings, or deeds.

Islam and peace: Linguistically the word "Islam" in Arabic comes from the root word "salama," which means free of harm, and is related to the word "Salaam," which means peace.

> Muhammad defined a Muslim: "the one who does not harm other people. No harm comes from his tongue and hands [i.e. words and actions]."

 In Islam, "The Peace" is one of the magnificent names and attributes of God. The one who submits to God finds inner peace within him or herself and should be at peace with the environment and the people.

Muslims greet each other with the word *as-salaamu alaykum*, which means "peace be upon you," instead of the words "Hi" or "Hello." The full version of this statement is "peace be upon you as well as Allah's mercy and blessings."

Muslims or Muhammadans?: Unlike Chrisitans and Buddhists, the followers of Muhammad are not called Muhammadans. An adherent to Islam or the one who embraces it as a faith and a way of life is called a "Muslim," i.e. the one who believes in and submits to God.

The six elements of the Islamic creed: The belief in one God requires the belief in His Angels, His Books, His Messengers, as well as the belief in the Day of Judgment and the belief in God's Divine Pre-ordainment.

Pillars of Islam-practicing the Islamic faith:

The Islamic religion is based on five pillars that a Muslim must practice:

1	Shahadah	Uttering the creed of Islam (there is no God but Allah and Muhammad is a messenger of Allah)
2	Salat	Performing daily prescribed prayers
3	Siyam	Fasting for the lunar month of Ramadan
4	Zakat	Paying alms as charity once a year
5	Hajj	Pilgrimage to the Sacred Mosque (the House of God) in Mecca once in a lifetime for those who have the physical and financial ability

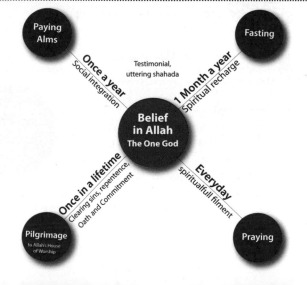

1. Uttering the Creed of Islam, Shahadah:

This is to acknowledge that there is one and only one God to be worshiped. He created the universe and all beings. His name is Allah, and Muhammad is His messenger.

A person is said to be a Muslim when he or she believes in heart and utters the statement of *shahadah*: "I tesitify there is no deity but God and Muhammad is a Messenger of God."

[In Arabic it is spelled *ashadu'anna la ilaha illa Allah, wa ashadu'anna Muhammadan rasul 'Allah*].

Acknowledging Muhammad as a Prophet and a Messenger of God requires the acknowledgement of all Prophets and messengers God sent before him.

This is a testimony in Arabic calligraphy which was designed in an artistic way. It states: I witness that there is no God except Allah and Muhammad is His servant and His messenger.

2. Prescribed Daily Prayers:

Prayer (*salat*) in Islam is an act of worship that enables the individual to get intimately close to God. There are five daily-prescribed prayers in Islam that are distributed during the whole day cycle. The essence of worship is to glorify, exalt, and praise God with the heart, tongue, and body.

Islam..
Faith in
Action

	Fajr	Zuhr	Asr	Maghrib	Isha
	Before sunrise prayer	Sunrise	Noon prayer	Afternoon prayer	Sunset prayer	Evening prayer

> *And when My servants ask you, concerning Me —
> indeed I am near. I respond to the invocation of the
> supplicant when he or she calls upon Me. So let them
> respond to Me and believe in Me that they may be
> [rightly] guided.*
>
> *Surah 2:186*

Powerful Meditation

In fact, the word *salat* literally means "hot connection." It is a practical demonstration of faith. Each prayer includes physical movements of bowing and prostrating to God. Prayers show progressively increasing levels of submission to Allah. It requires full concentration and isolation from worldly matters. Prophet Muhammad said "a person is closest to God during prostration."

Praying five times a day may seem excessive to some people. In reality, it is a type of meditation that does not take more than forty minutes a day. Just as we must eat several times a day to gain physical nourishment, so too must we spiritually nourish our souls. Doing *salat* at spaced intervals throughout the day provides such spiritual nourishment.

3. Zakat, Alms Giving:

Zakat is an essential pillar of Islam. It means giving alms (paying a charity) once every year to poor, needy, and other rightful beneficiaries as stipulated by the Qur'an. It is specified that 2.5% of excess personal wealth must be given.

2.5% of Annual Net Savings

Zakat cleanses ones' heart from greed and removes hatred and jealousy from the hearts of the poor. It fosters social integration and collaboration, compassion, and respect. It enhances the well-being of the whole society and achieves social justice.

4. Fasting in Ramadan:

Muslims are required to fast for the whole lunar month of Ramadan (29 or 30 days), from the break of dawn to sunset. During the fasting time, Muslims are required to abstain from eating, drinking, and sexual contact while practicing a normal life.

Fasting for the sake of Allah helps to acknowledge that the sustenance which may be taken for granted actually comes directly from Allah.

When people feel the pangs of hunger, they experience the suffering needy people go through. The rich will be more inclined to give to charity when they fast. This builds up a relationship between the rich and the poor and helps build social harmony.

Fasting enables one to curb the inner desires, learn self-control, and, in doing so, achieve better spiritual development. Fasting has many health benefits and doctors recommend it to cure some diseases.

5. Pilgrimage to Mecca, Hajj:

Hajj is the pilgrimage to Mecca at the lunar month of Zul Hijjah with the intention to visit the Sacred Mosque (House of Allah) and perform certain religious rites. It is the fifth pillar of Islam that must be done once in a lifetime by all Muslims who have reached the age of puberty, provided they have the financial and physical ability to do it.

Prophecy

Lunar Months	
1	Al-Muharram
2	Safar
3	Rabi' Al-Awal
4	Rabi' Al-Akharah
5	Jumada Al-Oula
6	Jumada Al-Akharah
7	Rajab
8	Sha'ban
9	**Ramadan**
10	Shawwal
11	Zul Qui'da
12	**Zul Hijjah**

As people from all races and nations gather at the spiritual epicenter of the Islamic world, they are affirm their common paternal ancestry with Adam and their spiritual ancestry with Abraham

One God, One Message

The prophets and messengers of God in the Holy Qur'an:

Islam acknowledges all prophets and messengers God sent to the peoples of the Middle East before Muhammad for the guidance of humanity. Each prophet confirmed one message, "monotheism," which is the belief in God's existence and oneness.

God sent them to educate people about the purpose of life, protect them from falling astray, and teach them good morals.

The Qur'an mentions twenty-five prophets and messengers by name and focuses on the stories of some of them. For example, in the Qur'an Adam is mentioned twenty-five times, Noah forty-three times, Abraham sixty-nine times, Moses 136 times, and Jesus twenty-five times.

Muhammad said: "My similitude in comparison with the other prophets before me, is that of a man who has built a house completely and excellently except for a place of one brick. When people see the house, they admire its beauty and say: how splendid the house will be if the missing brick is put in its place. So I am that brick, and I am the last of the Prophets." (Narrated by Bukhari 4.734, 4.735)

Verily We sent messengers before you, among them those of whom We have told you [their story], and some of whom We have not told you [their story]; and it was not given to any messenger that he should bring a sign except by God's leave.

Surah 40:78

Say: We have believed in God and that which is revealed unto us and that which was revealed unto Abraham, and Ishmael, and Isaac, and Jacob and the tribes, and that which Moses and Jesus received, and that which the Prophets received from their Lord. We make no distinction between any of them, and unto Him we have surrendered.

Surah 2:136

Torah, Gospel, and Qur'an are God's revelations to humankind: Believing in God's revealed Books before the Qur'an is an essential pillar of the Islamic faith. Muslims believe that the Qur'an does not contradict the previous revelations, but that it points out and corrects deviations from truth that have happened through the history.

We did reveal the Torah, where in it there is guidance and a light.
Surah 5:44

And We sent following in their footsteps Jesus, the son of Mary, confirming that which came before him in the Torah, and We gave him the Gospel in which was guidance and light and confirmed that which preceded it of the Torah as guidance and instructions for the righteous.
Surah 5:46

And unto you [Muhammad] We revealed the Book with the truth, confirming whatever Scripture was before it, and a watcher over it.
Surah 5:48

Those whom God bestowed favor among the Prophets, of the descendents of Adam and of those whom We carried [in the ship] with Noah, and of the seed of Abraham and Israel, and from among those whom We guided and chose. When the revelations of The Beneficent were recited unto them, they fell in prostration, adoring and weeping.
Surah 19:58

The life of main prophets

Prophet	Muhammad	Jesus	Moses	Abraham
Approx. Period	570 - 632 CE	1-33 CE	around 1400 BC	around 1700 BC

Muhammad and Abraham:

Abraham is considered as the father of prophets in the Jewish, Christian, and Islamic religions because most of the known prophets were from his offspring. Muslims believe that prophet Muhammad is his descendent through his first son Ishmael who was also the father of many Arab tribes. On the other hand, the nation of Israel and many prophets such as Jacob, Joseph, Aaron, and Moses have descended from his second son Isaac.

Abraham dedicated his life and struggles to teaching people monotheism. The Qur'an frequently mentions Abraham and indicates that after he put an effort in searching for the truth and the oneness of God (The One Deity), Abraham proved his sincerity, honesty, thankfulness, and obedience to God. He presented one of the greatest and most memorable examples in history of full submission to God, even in the most difficult situations.

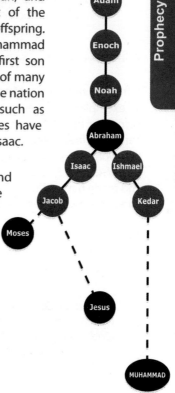

Prophecy

Adam — Enoch — Noah — Abraham — Isaac, Ishmael — Jacob, Kedar — Moses — Jesus — MUHAMMAD

> *Who is better in religion than the one who submits to*
> *God while being a doer of good and follows the religion*
> *of Abraham (inclining towards truth, the upright?*
> *And God chose Abraham as*
> *an intimate friend.*
>
> Surah 4:125

Abraham was a man of truth who showed an exemplary obedience to God, therefore, according to the Qur'an, God; chose Abraham as a friend and as one of the elite in the world and among the righteous in the Hereafter (4:125, 2:130). God guided him to the right religion and made him an "Imam," i.e. a leader for people (2:124) and described him as a nation (16:120).

One God

Abraham is revered by Muslims as the person who gave them their name as "Muslims" (i.e. those who believe in One God and submit to Him) (22:78).

> *Abraham was neither a Jew, nor a Christian; but he*
> *was "Musllman Hanifan," an upright man who had*
> *surrendered and sincerely submitted to God, and he*
> *was not of the idolaters.*
>
> Surah 3:67

The origin of the name "Abraham" was Abram or Avram and it is written and pronounced "Ibrahim" in Arabic. The Roman Catholic Church calls Abraham "our father in Faith." The Eastern Orthodox Church commemorates him as the "Righteous Forefather Abraham."

It is believed that the first building of worshipping one God was established when Adam first descended on the earth. Muslims believe that the person who rebuilt this building, and raised its walls was Prophet Abraham together with his son Ishmael. The building, which is cubical in shape, is called "Ka'bah." It is located in Mecca in the valley of Bacca (in Saudi Arabia). God imposed a duty upon Abraham and his son to purify the Ka'bah for those who pray, and prostrate to Him. God made it a place of worship, and a sanctuary (a safe place and a refuge) for the people.

Abraham and Ishmael's supplication:

> *"Our Lord! make us submissive unto You and of our Seed a nation submissive unto You, and show us our ways of worship, and accept our repentance. You are the Most Forgiving, the Most Merciful."*
> Surah 2:128

The Prophet Muhammad indicated that praying in the Sacred Mosque is highly rewardable. The reward for one prayer in the Sacred Mosque is equivalent to the reward of 100,000 prayers elsewhere.

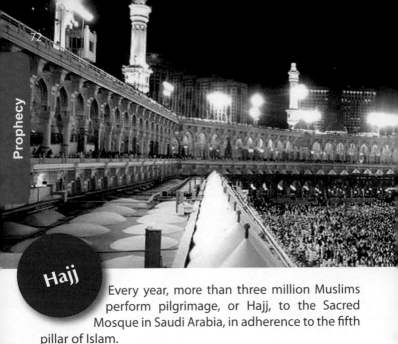

Prophecy

Hajj

Every year, more than three million Muslims perform pilgrimage, or Hajj, to the Sacred Mosque in Saudi Arabia, in adherence to the fifth pillar of Islam.

Muhammad taught people how to perform Hajj, which mainly contains Abrahamic rites. He circumambulated (walked in circles) around the Ka'bah, which is the cubical building established by Abraham as the House of God. Circulation is performed seven times and goes counterclockwise, as an act of submission to God which is also harmonious with the motion of the planets and even the electrons.

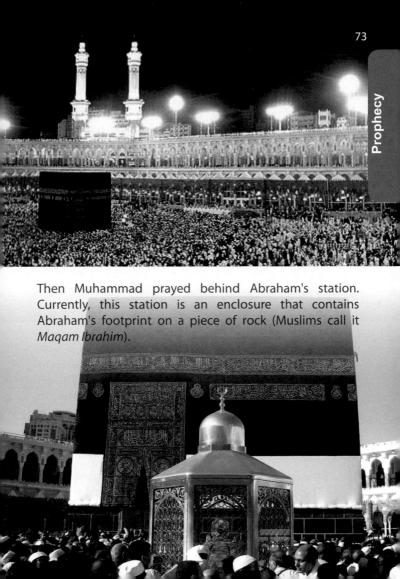

Then Muhammad prayed behind Abraham's station. Currently, this station is an enclosure that contains Abraham's footprint on a piece of rock (Muslims call it *Maqam Ibrahim*).

Then Muhammad walked between the Safa and Marwa hills, the same place Hagar walked thousands of years ago, searching for water after her husband Abraham left her there with their son Ishmael. Abraham asked her to stay there as an act of obedience and submission to the command of God, Who wanted the place to become a sanctuary and a place of worship.

The distance between these two hills is approximately 395m. This Hajj rite is called *sa'ee*, i.e. a brisk walk between the Safa and Marwa hills. It consists of seven laps with a total distance of 2.76 km, starting from Safa and finishing

at Marwa. *Sa'ee* resembles the daily motion, activities, actions, travel, effort, and acts a person performs during his or her life. These acts and deeds should be for useful and valuable goals. They must comply with God's Commandments.

In addition to other Hajj rites, Muhammad went to a place currently known as Jamarat in a town called Mina (8 km east of Mecca). There, he threw stones in resemblance of Abraham's act, when he stoned the Satan who appeared to him as an old man trying to dissuade him from slaughtering his son as a sacrifice to God. Abraham stoned him several times.

When Muslims perform the same act, they in fact challenge Satan and the evil desires within themselves.

Finally, as God saved Abraham's son and instead substituted a ram, Muhammad taught Muslims to provide a sacrifice to God by slaughtering a sheep or a goat as a symbol of Abraham's sacrifice, and divide the meat among the poor.

Muhammad taught Muslims to dedicate a supplication for Abraham and his family in each of the five daily prayers. Also, it is worth mentioning that Muhammad named one of his children—who died in his childhood—Ibrahim.

Say [O Muhammad]: My Lord has guided me to a straight path, a correct religion, the way and community of Abraham, the upright way inclining towards the truth and he was not an idolater.
Surah 6:161

It is believed that Abraham was buried in Hebron, Palestine. It is considered a sacred place for Jews, Christians, and Muslims. The building complex that contains the cenotaph of Abraham is called *Al-Masjid Al-Ibrahimi* (Abraham's Mosque). It is referred to as "Tombs of the Patriarchs" by non-Muslims.

The building is primarily a large mosque with two square minarets. It also includes many rooms and a series of subterranean caves.

The central room of the building contains the ceno-taphs of Abraham and his wife Sarah. The southern room (*Ohel Yitzhak* in Hebrew) contains the cenotaphs of Isaac and Rebecca.

The northern room of the building contains the cenotaphs of Jacob and Leah. It is widely believed the remnants of Abraham, Isaac, Jacob, Sarah, Rebecca, and Leah were enshrined in the subterranean chambers below the building.

Cenotaph of Abraham

Note: Muslims do not glorify tombs. According to Islamic teachings, the structure of the tomb must not be raised above the ground level.

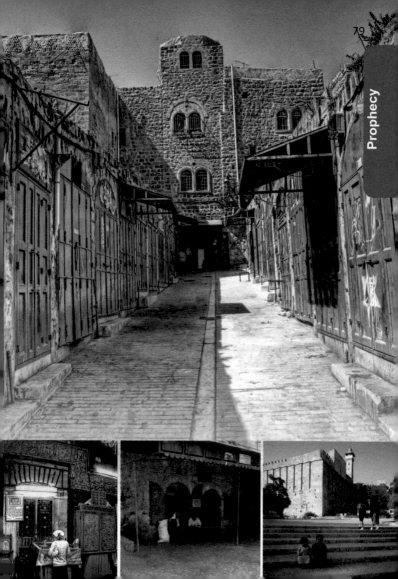

The Man Who Spoke to God

Muhammad and Moses:

Muhammad praised highly the Prophet Moses and indicated that on the Day of Resurrection he will see Moses standing and touching the side of the Throne of God.

On another occasion when Muhammad came to Medina and found that Jews fasted on the day of Ashura (on which God saved the children of Israel from the Pharaoh of Egypt), he asked Muslims to fast this day voluntarily because Moses fasted that day as an expression of thanks to God. The day of Ashura is on the tenth of the first month of the lunar calendar.

Approximately one third of the Qur'an talks about Moses and the experiences the children of Israel went through. In addition, the Qur'an mentions some of the prophets who were sent to the children of Israel, such as Aaron, Zachariah, and John.

The Qur'an indicates that God spoke to Moses and describes Moses as one of five messengers and prophets who had heavy missions and from whom God took a solemn covenant. The five messengers are Noah, Abraham, Moses, Jesus, and Muhammad, peace be upon all of them.

Moses died near or at Mount Nebo which overlooks the Dead Sea and the land of Palestine. A memorial was built on the mountain and has since become an important tourist attraction in Jordan.

حراسة الأراضي المقدسة
جبل نيبو ـ صياغة
مقام النبي موسى

MOUNT NEBO SIYAGHA
MEMORIAL OF MOSES

Muslims see many similarities between Moses and Muhammad. Both were prophets and messengers who brought a divine Book that included God's Law and Commandments. Both lead their people and lived among them for a long period of time. Both married and had children.

Muhammad and Jesus:

According to authentic reports, Muhammad said:

> "I am the nearest of all the people to the son of Mary and all the prophets are paternal brothers, and there has been no prophet between me and him (viz. Jesus)."

The Qur'an describes Jesus as "God's Word" and "glad tidings" conveyed to Mary. His name in the Qur'an is "The Messiah, Jesus son of Mary."

Jesus in the Qur'an

God supported him with the Holy Spirit (Archangel Gabriel) and sent him as a messenger to the children of Israel to guide them to the straight path and to worship God his Lord and their Lord and the Lord of all beings (see, 2:87, 3:45-9, 4:171).

Prophecy

Nazareth is a historic town in lower Galilee, Palestine. Mentioned in the Gospels as the home of Mary, it is closely associated with the childhood of Jesus Christ. According to Roman Catholic tradition, Annunciation took place at the Church of the Annunciation in Nazareth.

Also, the Qur'an describes Jesus as illustrious in the world and the Hereafter, and one of the righteous and those brought near unto God.

The Qur'an also indicates that God taught Jesus the scripture and wisdom, and the Torah and the Gospel. God supported him with miracles of healing the blind and the leper, and raising the dead by His leave and Will.

Photos from Bethlehem: The Church of the Nativity is one of the oldest operating churches in the world. It is believed by many Christians to mark the birthplace of Jesus the Christ.

The story of Mary and Jesus in the Qur'an

And mention Mary in the Scripture, when she had withdrawn from her people to an eastern place as a seclusion from them. Then We sent unto her Our spirit (Angel Gabriel) who appeared to her as a flawless human being.

She said: I seek refuge from you to God, the Beneficent One if at all you fear Him.
He said: I am none other than a messenger of your Lord to grant you a pure boy.
She said: How shall I have a boy [son] and neither a human being has ever touched me nor have I been unchaste!
He said: So it will be. Your Lord said: It is easy.

Surah 19: 16-23

According to the story mentioned in the Qur'an, Mary brought her son to her own people who blamed her, but the newborn Jesus miraculously spoke and said (Surah 19: 30-35):

Indeed, I am the servant of God. He decreed to give me the Scripture and make me a prophet and make me blessed wherever I may be. And He enjoined me to pray to him and give alms as long as I am alive and to be virtuous towards my mother. He didn't make me insolent or wretched. May all peace be upon me the day I was born and the day I will die and the day I shall be raised alive.
That is Jesus son of Mary; it is the truth concerning what they doubt. It is not for God to take any son (Exalted Be He). When He decrees a matter, He but says to it: Be, and so it is.

Islam, a Universal Religion

Muslims believe that Muhammad received the same Message that was given to Abraham, Moses, Jesus, and other prophets, but his mission was universal. He was entrusted to correct people's beliefs, bring them back to the true faith, and teach them good deeds.

> *And We have not sent you but as a mercy to the worlds.*
> Surah 21:107

Muhammad's Letter to the Roman Emperor

Muhammad sent letters to the rulers and kings of neighboring countries and superpowers such as Persia, Byzantine, and Egypt, calling them to accept Islam as "the Message of God." When Heraclius King of Byzantine received Muhammad's letter, he invited Abu-Sufyan (one of the main chiefs and tradesmen of Mecca who was by chance doing business in that area) to attend him. Heraclius asked Abu-Sufyan a few questions and requested that he be honest.

Letter of Prophet Muhammad to Heraclius (in original Arabic alphabets)

Heraclius : Which social class of the society does Muhammad come from?

Abu-Sufyan : He comes from a noble family in Mecca.

Heraclius : Did he ever betray, break a promise, or lie?

Abu-Sufyan : No.

Heraclius : How about his followers, are they increasing or decreasing? And have any of his followers quit because they were not pleased with Muhammad?

Abu-Sufyan : In fact, Muhammad's followers admire him and they are increasing in number.

Heraclius : Then what does Muhammad teach his followers?

Abu-Sufyan : Belief in One God and social justice.

Heraclius thought for a while, then said: "If what you told me is true, then Muhammad will be able to inherit my kingdom."

Emperor Heraclius ruled the Roman Empire from 610 to 640 CE. During that time he conducted three military campaigns, and defeated the Persian Empire and regained Syria, Palestine, and Egypt. In year 636, Islam reached Palestine, Syria, Egypt, and most of Northern Africa. In the year 642, Islam reached Persia.

Currently Islam is the second largest religion in the world. A comprehensive demographic study of more than 200 countries finds that there are 1.57 billion Muslims of all ages living in the world today, representing 23% of an estimated 2009 world population of 6.8 billion (Pew Forum on Religion & Public Life 2009).

Not all Muslims are Arabs: Arab Muslims constitute less than one fourth of the total number of Muslims in the world.

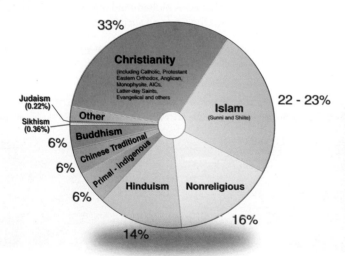

There are approximately 2.1 billion Christians in the world representing 33% of World's population, and 1.1 billion non religious/atheist people in the world (16% of world's population). Judaism represents 0.22% of the world'spopulation (about 14 million people).

Photo taken from the Grand Sultan Qaboos Mosque, Sultanate of Oman. Fine Islamic Architecture is reflected through the timber ceilings, Islamic arches, and wall decorations.

Chapter 5

The Islamic Civilization
Values and Morals

وانك لعلى خلق عظيم

You are of great moral character
Surah 68:4

Muhammad and the Promotion of Values

The role of religion in public life is a hotly contested subject. Even though today there is a clear separation of religious and secular spheres (a recent development in Europe and America), the influence of religion is easy to see and plays a roll in civil society debates on family life, public education, health care, war and peace, stewardship of the environment, foreign policy, and more.

In the Muslim world, religious values and teachings have continued to be central in how Muslims go about their daily lives. One of the prevalent myths about Islam is that there is no separation between mosque and state in the Muslim world. It is true that Muhammad was both prophet and statesmen. However, once Islam spread widely and became the dominant religion between Europe and Asia, it developed a complex political and cultural system that had clear distinctions between the religious sphere in society, overseen by religious scholars, and the political sphere, headed by ruling figures and an administrative class that included many non-Muslims.

The genius of Islamic civilizations was its ability to bring together so many different cultures through the Quranic teachings on how humans should treat each other and how society should be based on universal values.

The founders of all great religions provide their followers with beautiful examples of how to live a righteous life. With Muhammad, Muslims have rich historical details from their beloved Prophet, who lived a very public life as a religious leader, husband, father, business man, grandfather, and more. Muslims turn to the Qur'an and to the life of Muhammad for inspiration in leading a God-centered life.

Muhammad encouraged people to love one another:

Muhammad said, "I swear by God that you will not be true believers in Him unless you love each other. I will tell you something that if you do it you will love each other: Greet each other frequently and make it a common habit."

And he said, "No one will become a good believer unless he wishes for his brethren what he likes for himself."

And further Muhammad told his followers: "Whoever helps a believer overcome a difficulty, God will help him overcome a difficulty on the Day of Judgment, and God will always help an individual as long as he or she is helping others."[1]

Acts of kindness and friendly greetings:
Muhammad said, "Don't underestimate the
value of any simple kind act, even if you
only meet others with a bright and smiling
face."[2] And he said to someone who asked
him about a good way to deal with people:
"Offer people food and greet who you know
and who you don't know."[3]

"Meeting others
with a brigh,
smiling face is an
act of charity."

Muhammad ﷺ

Values & Morals

It is also reported that Muhammad used to
meet people with a bright face, and when
he shook hands with others, he never released his hand
before the other person.

Muhammad enjoyed life and had a keen sense of humor:
Muhammad was a complex figure. He was dignified
and serious, but he also had a great sense of humor. He
was cheerful and optimistic. People who dealt with him
described him as someone who cared for others deeply
and wanted them to feel good about themselves and life
in general.

On several occasions he joked with his friends, his
wife, elders in the community, and with children. In
Muhammad's day, running races was a common activity
for fun. Muhammad was often seen racing with his wife,
his children, and other children. There is a sweet story that
shows the Prophet's sense of humor and enjoyment of
running:

His wife Aisha reports that, "I went out with the Prophet on a journey. At that time I was a young girl and was quite slender. The Prophet told the people, 'Go on ahead,' so they went ahead, then he said to me, 'Come, let us have a race.' So I raced with him, and I won. He let the matter rest until I had gained weight. Later, I accompanied him on another journey. He told the people, 'Go on ahead,' so they went ahead. He said to me, 'Come, let us have a race.' So I raced with him, and he won. He began to laugh, and said, 'This is for that.'"

Muhammad cared for and loved children: There are many stories of Muhammad taking special care with children in his community. He used to greet them and play games with them. Once, the Prophet saw a little boy named Umayr who was sad because his little bird had died. Although Muhammad was heading elsewhere, he spent some time with the boy, and asked him sweetly with a rhyming play on words what had happened to Umayr's *nughayr* (the name for that kind of bird). This act of care and kindness from the Prophet brought some consolation to the child.

Muhammad often spoke to parents about their treatment of children. In his day, treatment of children, and especially young girls, was often harsh. Boys were valued more and there was a practice of taking baby girls in the desert to die. In the Qur'an this practice is denounced emphatically and it speaks with righteous indignation of *"when the girl-child buried alive is asked what she did to deserve murder" (Surah 81:8-9)*.

Muhammad urged parents to express their love to their children by kissing and hugging them and being fair with all of them, boys and girls. He described a father who never kissed his child as lacking in mercy in his heart.

Muhammad loved his neighbors and urged everyone to practice compassion toward others: Muhammad had a Jewish neighbor who did not accept Islam and who was not particularly kind to the Prophet. When this neighbor became sick, Muhammad visited him at his home, seeing what he could do to help. This kindness softened the man's heart. There was also a Jewish boy who at times helped out in Muhammad's home. When the boy became sick, Muhammad went to visit him and check on his health.

Muhammad told his companions that the Angel Gabriel urged all people to be good neighbors. This was such a point of emphasis in Muhammad's life that the Prophet thought that someone might even inherit from a neighbor if so designated in a will, something that broke with Arab custom.

Be Kind to Your Neighbours

One day Muhammad instructed one of his companions as follows: "If you cook soup, cook it with more water [to increase its amount] so there will be enough to share with your neighbors."

Muhammad urged all to abandon all rude behavior:

On several occasions, the Prophet made it clear that the people of good morals are the closest to him on the Day of Judgment and will be most beloved by him. He also made it clear what he expected of Muslims: "Don't hate each other and don't envy each other, and be brothers."[4]

"A believer in God does not curse or swear or use bad language."[5]

These moral demands are elaborations on how to live out the Golden Rule. Muhammad emphasized this to his companions by reciting to them the following verses from the Qur'an:

The believers are a band of brothers. Make peace among your brothers and fear God, so that you may be shown mercy.

O believers! Let no man mock another man ... Let no woman mock another woman .... Do not defame one another, nor call one another by nicknames. It is an evil thing to be called by a bad name after embracing the true Faith. Those that do not repent are wrongdoers.

Believers, avoid immoderate suspicion, for in some cases suspicion is a sin. Do not spy on one another, nor backbite one another. Would any of you like to eat the flesh of his dead brother? Surely you would loathe it. Have fear of God. God is forgiving and merciful.

Surah 49:10-12

Don't spread false reports:

O believers! If an evildoer brings you a piece of news, inquire first into its truth, lest you should wrong others unwittingly and then regret your action.

Surah 49:6-7

Don't cheat others. and be honest: Trading, buying, and selling should be based on ethics. Muhammad always insisted that Muslims should demonstrate their faith in their interactions with others whether it be doing business or in personal affairs:

"Whoever cheats is not one amongst us."[6]

Lying or breaking a promise is hypocrisy:

The Prophet said:

"Whoever has the following four characteristics will be a hypocrite and whoever has one of them will have one characteristic of hypocrisy until he gives it up:

❶ Whenever he is entrusted, he betrays

❷ Whenever he speaks, he tells a lie

❸ Whenever he makes a covenant, he proves treacherous

❹ Whenever he quarrels, he behaves in a very imprudent, evil, and insulting manner."

Muhammad condemned extremism:

Muhammad called for a balanced way of life that relies on rational thinking. There is a story from his life that is very telling of the Prophet's way when it comes to religion. The story goes that three men came to Muhammad's house to ask about how he worshipped. Muhammad was not at home and his wife spoke to the men and answered their questions about the Prophet's religious practice. They found Muhammad's level of worship to be less than they expected.

According to their understanding, to be truly religious requires a more ascetic way of life, ignoring some bodily needs to purify body and mind from desires. They thought they needed to remain unmarried and celibate. They also thought that devout Muslims needed to fast every day and perform extra prayers late at night in addition to the five daily prayers.

When Muhammad returned home and heard of the discussion and the views of these early Muslim zealots, he was not pleased. He said that he often performed extra prayers at night but that he also got his sleep like other people. In addition to fasting during Ramadan, he sometimes fasted at other times, but he did not recommend perpetual fasting. And finally he encouraged marriage and family life; he was, of course, married and a father and grandfather. The Prophet made it clear:

"This is my *sunnah* (the way approved by God). Whoever does not accept it is not one of us."[7]

Finding balance between body and soul: On several occasions, Muhammad called on Muslims to find the right balance between the demands of living in the material world and the spiritual needs of the soul.

The Prophet felt that it was essential to live a life of moderation. He encouraged people to use religion as a complete way of life that addresses material and spiritual needs; that religion can guide each of us to make positive changes in our lives in a way that brings peace to our hearts and to our families and communities. Muhammad wanted people to find peace and wellness in this life and not to live as ascetics. He encouraged people to look after their bodies and to eat in moderation.

Muhammad encouraged sport and recreation: Muhammad often encouraged his companions to maintain healthy bodies and to participate in different types of sports, such as swimming, archery, horsemanship.

As we noted earlier, Muhammad himself enjoyed running competitions with his companions and family members. The Prophet even set aside an area on the western side of the Prophet's Mosque in Medina for races. Another mosque was built on the other side of the race course and was called the Sabaq Mosque, or "the mosque of the racing field."

The value of knowledge

One of the sayings of Muhammad's that show how important seeking knowledge was to him:

"Seeking knowledge is obligatory upon every Muslim (male and female)."[8]

Muhammad brought a message of light and guidance that became the source for great advancements in science and civilization for many centuries. The Qur'an and sayings of Muhammad stress acquiring knowledge through observation of nature and exploring the world.

The words *read, think, learn, observe, explore, ponder, contemplate,* and *reflect,* are often used in the Qur'an.

And say: My Lord, increase me in knowledge.
Surah: 20:114

In the creation of the heavens and the earth, and in the alternation of night and day, there are signs for those of understanding; those who remember God when standing, sitting, and lying down, and reflect on the creation of the heavens and the earth, saying: "Our Lord, You have not created this in vain."

Surah 3:190-191

And in the earth there are wondrous signs and also in yourselves, can you not see them?

Surah 51:20-21

Muhammad encouraged people to learn and seek useful knowledge:
He urged his companions to use their knowledge for the well-being of humanity and not to cause harm. He linked this pursuit of knowledge to God's pleasure when he said:

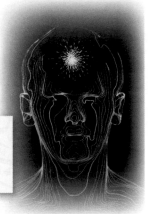

"Who follows a way for acquiring knowledge, God facilitates a way for him to Paradise."

For many centuries, Muslim scientists were leaders in exploring the frontiers of pure and applied sciences. Arabic, the language of the Qur'an, became the language of the most advanced scientific research in medicine, astronomy, mathematics, engineering, geography, and chemistry from Spain to Asia. In Europe, scientific research lagged behind Islamic civilization.

Beginning in Spain, Christian scholars and scientists benefited from the translation of both Greek and Arabic philosophical and scientific texts made by Muslim scientists and scholars.

The prominent historian of science Charles Singer notes that in regards to scientific and technological development in the pre-modern world, "the Near East was superior to the West. For nearly all branches of technology, the best products available to the West were those of the Near East. Technologically, the West had little to bring to the East. The technological movement was in the other direction."[9]

Values & Morals

Scientist	Major Contributions
Geber Father of Chemistry **721-815 CE**	**Jaber Ibn Hayyan** was a prominent polymath: a chemist, astronomer, astrologer, engineer, geologist, philosopher, physicist, and pharmacist and physician. He is considered by many scientists to be the father of chemistry. He was the first to discover many acids such as nitric, hydrochloric, and sulfuric acids. He described many chemical processes, such as evaporation, sublimation, and distillation. The historian of chemistry Erick John Holmyard gives credit to Geber for developing alchemy into an experimental science.
Algoritmi Father of Algorithms **780-850 CE**	**Mohammad Ibn Musa Al-Khwarizmi** was one of the greatest scientists of his time. He was a mathematician, an astronomer and a geographer. He introduced the decimal positional number system to the world. He made a great contribution to Mathematics when he developed Algebra (derived from the word Al-Jabr) and "algorithms," to which he gave his name. His name is the origin of the word guarismo in Spanish and the word *algarismo* in Portuguese, both meaning digit.
Rhases (Rasis) Father of Physicians **865-929 CE**	**Abu Bakr Muhammad Ibn Zakariya Al-Razi**. He was considered by many scientists as the father of physicians. He was the first to differentiate smallpox from measles. He discovered numerous compounds and chemicals, including alcohol and kerosene. E. G. Browne considers him as the most original of all the physicians. He wrote many important books—which were translated to different languages including English—such as the nine-volume medical encyclopedia, *Al-Hawi*, and the first book on pediatrics, *The Diseases of Children*.

Avicenna Father of Modern Medicine **980-1037 CE**	**Abu Ali Al-Hussein Ibn Sina** is one of the most eminent Muslim scholars in medicine and one of the most famous Muslim scientists in the world. He was a polymath and the author of almost 200 books on science, religion, and philosophy. Avicenna's two most important works are: *Al-Shifa* (*The Book of Healing*), which is a philosophical encyclopedia based on Aristotelian tradition, and *Al-Qanun Fi-Tibb* (*The Canon of Medicine*). *The Canon* is a 14-volume book which classifies and describes diseases, and outlines their assumed causes. It was translated to different languages and was a standard medical text in Europe for seven centuries (until early eighteenth century).
Al Jazari **1136-1206 CE**	**Abul-Iz Bin Ismael Al-Jazari**. He is best known for writing the *Book of Knowledge of Ingenious Mechanical Devices* where he described fifty mechanical devices along with instructions on how to construct them. Al-Jazari is also known as the inventor of the largest astronomical "castle clock," which is considered to be the first programmable analog computer. According to Donald Routledge Hill, Al-Jazari described the most sophisticated candle clocks. He also invented the water clock and the crank shaft that transforms rotary motion into linear motion.

LATIN FIGURES:

I, II, III, IV, V, VI, VII, VIII, IX, X

ARABIC NUMBERS :

0, 1, 2, 3, 4, 5, 6, 7, 8, 9, 10

Avicenna

Bringing religious values to trade and commerce: As we saw earlier, Muhammad was a business man in partnership with his wife, Khadijah. Together they were involved in the trading of goods. Not surprisingly, the Prophet had many things to say about how people should conduct their business affairs.

Muhammad never tired of stressing the importance of value-based action in every sphere of human endeavor. In business he made it clear that any form of cheating, unethical dealings, deception, fraud, monopoly, and exploitation is unlawful and a sin. When people conduct their business affairs fairly and with justice, society benefits and this leads to spiritual benefits to the righteous businessman and woman. Thus Muhammad said:

"God betows his mercy on a person who is tolerant when he buys, tolerant when he sells, and tolerant when he asks for his rights."[11]

Soon after Muhammad arrived in Medina, he instructed his companions to buy a piece of land and dedicate it for free trade. People used to buy and sell in this market without paying any fees or custom charges. They called it Manakha.

The land has been left as an endowment and is still in use today. The picture at the bottom of this page shows the wall surrounding the designated free trade market.

Manakha means the place where camels are seated on the ground in order to off load goods carried on their backs (for trade purposes).

Expressing values through etiquette: Muhammad was known for his high sense of decorum and practice of good manners, or etiquette. He taught his companions that etiquette is part of his example and way of life, his *sunnah*. In addition, many verses of the Qur'an urge believers to exhibit tenderness and good manners. Here are the essentials of what has become the hallmark of Islamic etiquette, based on the teachings of the Qur'an and the example of Muhammad:

- Do not talk loudly and do not arrogantly.
- Do not stay long when visiting a sick person, give him or her time to rest.
- One should smell good when attending mosque.
- Do not attend mosque if you have recently eaten onions or garlic, so as not to disturb others.
- Be helpful and give space to others in crowded areas where finding space is difficult.
- Call others by the names and nicknames that they like.
- Put your hand on your mouth when yawning and bless others when they sneeze.
- When talking to others, use the good words to them. A good word is like an alm or charity in Islam.

- Talk kindly to your parents and don't shout at their faces, never say a bad word, even uff or fee (the smallest negative words in Arabic).
- Children should always knock on the door and seek permission before entering their parents' room.
- If you are serving water to others, you are the last one to drink.
- If you are invited to dinner or a banquet, eat from the closer serving dishes to you so as not to annoy others near you.
- Do not stare at people, but lower your gaze, especially men should do this for women to make women feel safe.

Purification and cleanliness: The old truism is that "cleanliness is next to Godliness." Muslims share this universal sentiment and have uniquely Islamic practices to ensure its occurrence. The Qur'an has many beautiful verses encouraging purity and cleanliness

> *God loves those who purify themselves.*
> Surah 9:108
>
> *God does not wish to burden you. He seeks only to purify you and to perfect His favor to you, so that you may give thanks.*
> Surah 5:6
>
> *"Truly God loves those who ask for forgiveness and strive to keep themselves clean.*
> Surah 2:222

The practice of purification is made every time Muslims pray. Performing ablutions (*wudu'*) before praying is an essential aspect of this fundamental Muslim rite. It includes washing the hands, face, forearms up to the elbows, wiping the head and washing the feet.

Ablutions Everyday

Muhammad emphasized cleanliness and purification in all aspects of life. He asked his companions to clean their homes and surroundings regularly. He taught them that removing harm or garbage from the road is a noble act of charity. The Prophet also urged his followers to maintain their hygiene and cleanliness. His sayings on this topic indicate the following:

- Dress in clean and tidy clothes but do not be extravagant
- Use perfumes or colognes (teeb) to smell good
- Trim your nails, remove pubic and armpit hair
- Wash your hands before and after eating. Do not touch food after waking up until your hands are washed.
- Take good dental care by brushing teeth prior to each daily prayer.

Respect other points of view: Whenever the Prophet gave instructions to his followers that were understood in two different ways, he would accept both ways, as long as both of them achieved the required goal in a lawful manner.

In one of the battles against the Meccans, the Muslim commander Amr bin Al-Aass was criticized for leading a prayer without performing not just the ablutions but also the full body wash known as *ghusul* (i.e., he was in a state of spiritual impurity). Muhammad listened to his justification. Amr told Muhammad that it was cold that night and if he showered he might fall sick and could not serve as commander. On hearing Amr's words, he accepted the commander's decision.

Muhammad was realistic and easy to deal with: This attitude of doing what is sensible was a trademark of Muhammad's. Another companion, Anas bin Malik said that he served the Prophet for ten years and was never asked, "Why did you do that?"

The word Muhammad in Arabic, designed in an artistic way. Courtesy of Artist Farid Al-Ali.

Values & Morals

Muhammad encouraged consultation and democracy (*shura*): Today there is a vigorous debate going on about the role of democracy in Islamic majority countries. Muhammad always consulted with his companions and his wife. He advised his followers to be objective and use rational thinking. Even though he was revered as the Messenger of God, Muhammad empowered his companions and involved them in the decision-making process. The Holy Quran, Surah 42:38 indicates:"...and conduct their affairs by consultation among themselves".

Consultation

When the Meccan chiefs, along with other Arab tribes, planned to attack Medina, the Persian Muslim named Salman suggested that the Muslims dig a trench on the north side of Medina. This was unheard of amongst the Arabs and was being advanced by a non-Arab. Muhammad considered the trench and discussed it with his men. The majority approved of the tactic and it saved the day.

At the Battle of Badr, one of the Muslims not part of the leadership group said to Muhammad: "O Prophet, if your choice to camp in this area is not inspired by a revelation, can I suggest we move to another area?" The Muslim put forward the reasons for his suggestion and after consultation Muhammad welcomed the proposal and they relocated the troops and gained tactical advantage.

Muhammad urged respect for people of other faiths: The Prophet encouraged his companions to be friendly and open with people of other religions while remaining firm in their Islamic faith. As we saw earlier, Islam began in turmoil, with intense persecution of the small Muslim community in Mecca by the pagan "nonbelievers" of the Quraysh tribe. Battles were fought in self-defense to keep the new faith and its oppressed followers from being wiped out. Quranic verses that speak of fighting and killing "nonbelievers" are addressed to this very specific historical moment and not to fighting and killing non-Muslims in general or especially Christians and Jews.

In fact, both the Qur'an and Muhammad repeatedly make clear that religion is a matter of individual conscience and that:

> *There shall be no compulsion in religion.*
> *True guidance is now distinct from error.*
> Surah 2:256

Other important verses in the Qur'an emphasize that Muhammad was called to deliver the divine message and people are then free to choose whether to believe or not:

> *Therefore give warning. Your duty is only to give warning:*
> *you cannot compel them.*
> Surah 88:21-22

> *But if they pay no heed, O Prophet, remember your mission*
> *is only to give clear delivery of the message entrusted to you.*
> Surah 16:82

The Qur'an also notes that different religious communities will have different ways of worship:

> *For every faith community We have ordained a ritual which they observe. Let them not dispute with you concerning this. Call them to the path of your Lord: you are rightly guided. If they argue with you, say: 'God knows best all that you do. On the Day of Resurrection God will judge your differences.*
>
> Surah 22: 67-69

It is clear that Muhammad had a high regard for Jesus and Christianity. He sent his vulnerable early followers to the Christian kingdom of Abyssinia for protection, and as we saw earlier, Muhammad revered Jesus and his mother Mary.

In 632 CE, Muhammad received and hosted at the mosque in Medina a Christian delegation from Najran in the Yemen. The Christians came to learn about Islam and to discuss the differences between Islam and Christianity. Muhammad set forth some guidelines for interfaith dialogue, emphasizing respect, wisdom, mutual understanding, and kindness. He recited to the assembled Muslims and Christians the following verse from the Qur'an:

Be courteous when you debate with the People of the Book, except with those among them who do wrong. Say: "We believe in that which has been revealed to us and which was revealed to you. Our God and your God is one. To Him we submit." Thus have We revealed the Book to you. Those to whom We gave the Scriptures believe in it, and so do some of your own people.

Surah 29: 46-47

Ex Grand Mufti of Bosnia Dr. Mustafa Ceric and Bishop Kevin Manning, Catholic Diocese of Parramatta. Sydney Australia 2007

Interfaith dialogue and peaceful coexistence with people of other faiths: Interfaith dialogue can be defined as open-ended communication and discussion between people of different faiths in order to reach positive outcomes. Beyond this, an even deeper level of interfaith dialogue comes when members of different religions share with each other their rituals and holy days. These acts of dialogue and participation in the interfaith prayer and service help to end suspicion and move people of faith from conflict to friendliness.

Religious Tolerance

The Omar Mosque and the Church of the Holy Sepulcher, Jerusalem: In the old city of Jerusalem, a great example of religious tolerance has existed for centuries. It started when the second Muslim ruler after Muhammad's death, the Caliph Omar bin Al-Khattab, entered Jerusalem peacefully from the Byzantines without spilling a drop of blood (638 CE).

Omar was invited by Sophronius, the Archbishop of Jerusalem, to pray in the Church of the Holy Sepulcher, also known as the Church of the Resurrection. It is the holiest Christian site in the world. It encompasses Calvary where Christians believe Jesus was crucified, and the tomb where he was buried. It has been an important pilgrimage destination for Christians since the fouth century of the Common Era.

In a remarkable gesture, Omar declined the Archbishop's invitation to pray in the church, saying, "If I prayed in the church it would have been taken by Muslims as a mosque for worship."

Omar prayed instead a few yards outside the church. His act confirmed the peaceful coexistence between Islam and other religions. It confirmed freedom of worship for non-Muslims under an Islamic state. A mosque was built on that site where Omar prayed and is called the Omar Mosque (that piece of land was donated for building the mosque).

The Covenant of Omar:

Omar granted the people of Jerusalem a covenant of peace and protection that became known as the Covenant of Omar. It has been mounted at the door of the mosque since the mosque's founding, and remains there to this day.

THE COVENANT OF OMAR

In the name of God, the Most Merciful, the Most Compassionate

This is an assurance of peace and protection given by the servant of God, Omar, to the people of Illia (Jerusalem). He gave them an assurance of protection for their lives, property, churches as well as the sick and healthy and all its religious community.

Their churches shall not be occupied, demolished nor taken away wholly or in part. None of their crosses nor property shall be seized. They shall not be coerced in their religion nor shall any of them be injured. None of the Jews shall reside with them in Ilia'.

The people of Illia' shall pay a tax (jizia) as inhabitants of cities do. They shall evict all Romans and thieves.

He whoever gets out shall be guaranteed safety for his life and property until he reaches his safe haven. He whoever stays shall be safe, in which case he shall pay as much tax as the people of Ilia do. Should any of the people of Ilia wish to move, together with his property, along with the Romans and to clear out of their churches and crosses, they shall be safe for their lives, churches, and crosses, until they have reached their safe haven. He whoever chooses to stay he may do so and he shall pay as much tax as the people of Ilia do. To the contents of this convent here are given the Covenant of God, the guarantees of His Messenger, the Caliphs, and the Believers, provided they (the people of Ilia) pay their due tax.

NOTES

1. *Riyad Al-Salihin, Sahih Al-Bukhari.*

2. *Riyad Al-Salihin.*

3. *Riyad Al-Salihin.*

4. *Sahih Al-Bukhari.*

5. *Sahih Al-Albani, Abu Dawood, Emam Ahmed,* and *Tirmidhi.*

6. *Riyad Al-Salihin, Bukhari.*

7. *Riyad Al-Salihin, Sahih Al-Bukhari.*

8. *Riyad Al-Salihin.*

9. Charles Singer, "Epilogue," in Charles Singer. et al. (eds), *A History of Technology,* Vol. II (Oxford: Oxford University Press, 1979), p. 756.

Photo by Peter Sanders

The Dome of the Rock, Jerusalem

Chapter 6

Women

Blue Mosque, Istanbul, Turkey

Muhammad, the Qur'an, and the Rights of Women

In one sense it is true to say that Muhammad led a spiritual revolution through his inspired ministry, confronting a corrupt and cruel sixth century Arab culture. Arabs call the time before Islam *jahiliyah*, or the "days of ignorance."

Still, Muhammad was dealing with human nature and entrenched customs, some good and some bad. He worked to change and improve an Arab society that fought against his reformation. As one Muslim scholar has noted, "Improvement and evolution, and not total revolution, was often the method of the Qur'an."[1]

Slavery, for example, was not ended, but freeing slaves was encouraged and the position of the slave in society was improved and protected. Women's rights were greatly enhanced through the teachings of the Qur'an and illustrated by the Prophet's example. In general, prior to Muhammad and the rise of Islam, women had no civil rights; they were more often than not male or tribal goods. Arabs gave preference to male over female babies to the extent that some fathers used to bury their infant daughters alive. This practice is denounced in the Qur'an as a grave injustice:

> *When the girl-child buried alive*
> *Is asked what she did to deserve murder...*
> *Then a soul will know what it has prepared.*
> Surah 81:8-9, 14

No gender discrimination: Muhammad condemned discrimination between male and female children and taught his companions to love their children and raise them properly regardless of gender. In fact, he emphasized giving more care and attention to female children. Muhammad said:

> "Women are the twin halves of men." [2]

Women inherit like men: Before Islam, women had no right to inherit. This was the case in many parts of the world. Muhammad successfully changed this custom. Muslim women gained the right to inherit like men. The Qur'an defined the portions for each individual (male and female) eligible to inherit.

The right to own property and control personal wealth was unheard of for women until very recently throughout the world. As Karen Armstrong notes, "The very idea that a woman could be a witness or could inherit anything at all in her own right was astonishing." [3]

Medieval Christians criticized Muslims for the rights given to women and slaves; and in the colonial period when many territories were placed under British rule and law, Muslim women lost property rights given to them by Islamic law.

Women have a unique identity: A woman is not considered a part of her husband's belongings. She has a unique identity. When a woman gets married, she does not need to change her surname. Her identity is preserved and her wealth and property are protected by Islamic law. When her husband dies, she is considered as one of the heirs and not a property inherited by male heirs.

Name
Surname
Middle Names

A woman is not a sex object: Prostitution and adultery are strictly forbidden in Islam. Muhammad made it clear that when a person— either man or woman—commits fornication or adultery he or she is not in a state of *imán*, or faithfulness.

> *And come not near unto adultery.*
> *Lo! it is an abomination and an evil way.*
> Surah 17:32

The word "Muhammad" in Arabic calligraphy, designed in an artistic and symmetrical way. The actual word looks like this 𝄢. Letters M and H, which form the first half of the word "Muhammad," are symmetrical with letters M and D which form the second half of the word "Muhammad" in Arabic.

How women dress is a topic that all cultures seem to obsess over. Fashion magazines, commercials, and advertisements in the West see female sexuality as a means to selling everything from toothpaste to cars. Islam takes a more conservative approach, with the underlying moral basis that human honor should be paramount and that there is harm to all of society when sexual exploitation is allowed and even promoted.

The Qur'an actually does not have a lot of specifics regarding how either men or women must dress. Most of the rules for dress were created within specific times and cultural moods. Fashion changes constantly, even in the Muslim world! But the Qur'an provides guidelines for Muslims. The Qur'an begins with a call to both men and women to observe modesty in dress and in behavior:

Tell the believing men to lower their gaze and to be mindful of their chastity: this will be most conducive to their purity—and, verily, God is aware of all that they do. And tell the believing women to lower their gaze and be mindful of their chastity, and not to display their charms in public beyond what may decently be apparent thereof. Hence, let them draw their head coverings over their bosoms. And let them not display more of their charms to any but their husbands or their fathers or their husbands' fathers, or their sons, or their sisters' sons.

Surah 24: 30-31

In Islam, tradition has held that this verse calls for women to wear what is known as *hijab*, the head covering that hides a woman's hair but reveals her face. In some parts of the world, even more covering of women is thought to be religiously required. In the United States, a Pew Research study reports that American Muslim women are evenly split between those who wear *hijab* as part of their everyday dress and those who don't wear hijab or only do so during prayer and at mosques. As part of a religion of nearly 1.5 billion followers spread all across the globe, Muslim approachs to modesty are diverse.

But what all Muslims agree on is that Quranic teachings call for modesty and non-sexist relations between men and women. Muslims, of course, struggle with these ideals as do all people regardless of religious affiliation. But the goal is clear: Islam calls for a way of life that prevents sexual harassment, sexual assault, rape crimes, and other behaviors that are harmful to individuals and society.

Muhammad empowered women:
Another way Muhammad strengthened and em-powered women was by allocating certain days every week for women's education. He urged them to participate in Islamic events, feasts, and prayers. Women and men prayed together in the Prophet's mosque, with the women praying together as a group behind the men. Even housemaids could meet Muhammad, talk to him, and seek his help and advice.

He also asked women to make a formal pledge (just as men did) since they are responsible for themselves to Islamic law.

Women play a crucial role in society as they nurture and raise the next generation to form the nation. Muslim women have been encouraged to take an active role in their society and continue to do so today.

Throughout the world, Muslim women are attending college in greater numbers and taking up leading roles in government, science, and industry. Muslim countries have had women presidents and prime ministers—this breakthrough has yet to occur in the United States. Although priority has always been given to the task of raising children and caring for their wellbeing, Muslim women have long worked and participated in the social and political life of their communities.

Muhammad encouraged full respect for mothers:

A man asked Muhammad, "Who deserves my closest support and companionship? Muhammad replied, "Your mother." Then the man asked Muhammad, who will be after her? Muhammad replied, "Your mother." The man asked the same question again and Muhammad replied for the third time, "Your mother." Then out of curiosity the man asked the same question a fourth time. To this, Muhammad said to him, "Your father."[5]

Muhammad encouraged caring for girls: Muhammad often emphasized the good treatment of females, and he described them as delicate and "fragile as glass." He told his companions that whoever raises his daughters properly, obeys God in caring for them, and guides them to faith, will gain Paradise.

Get married!

Muhammad encouraged people to get married and establish a family life. He taught his followers Islamic values that ban sexual relations outside of marriage.

Family Values

A young man once asked Muhammad to give him permission to have sex outside of marriage with a girlfriend or a prostitute. Muhammad replied, "Do you accept this for your mother?" The man answered, "No." Muhammad said, "Likewise, people don't like it for their mothers." Then he asked the young man three more times, "Do you like it for your daughter, sister, aunt?" Every time the man replied, "No," and Muhammad repeated the same statement: "Likewise, people don't like it for their daughters, sisters, and aunts."

Then Muhammad put his hand on the young man's heart and supplicated to God: "Oh my Lord, forgive his sin, purify his heart, and grant him chastity,"[4]

Muhammad encouraged good treatment of wives: Violence against women is all too often perpetrated by husbands. The World Health Organization (WHO) has found that violence against women—particularly spousal violence—is a major public health problem around the world. A WHO multi-country study found that between 15 to 17% of women aged 15-49 years reported physical and/ or sexual violence by an intimate partner at some point in their lives.[6]

Muhammad called on his male followers to abandon these horrible acts of violence in the family home.

He said, "The believers who show the most perfect faith are those who have the best character; and the best of the believers are those who are best to their wives."[7]

This promotes love, harmony, and mutual understanding, the bedrock of a good family and healthy societies.

Muhammad disliked divorce: He wanted all married couples to know the kind of happy marital life that he had. Should divorce become unavoidable, separation should be on good terms and with kindness [8].

Muhammad, Khadijah, and Aisha: A few years after his first wife, Khadijah, passed away, Muhammad married Aisha, the daughter of his closest friend, Abu-Bakr. Despite his loyalty to his late wife, he loved Aisha dearly and was honest to her.

Confirm your love to your wife: Aisha narrated that Muhammad described his love to her like a knot firmly tied in a rope. Aisha used to ask Muhammad from time to time, "How is the knot?" And Muhammad would confirm his love for her. He said, "The knot is still tied as firmly as it used to be."

Muhammad often asked Aisha to send a serving of food to the friends of his late wife Khadijah every time Aisha cooked a sheep or ewe.

Muhammad mentioned that no one was better than Khadijah in her time: she believed him when he first received God's revelations, when even Muhammad was unsure of their meaning, and when family members turned against him. In this moment it was Khadijah who offered support without any hesitation.

Muhammad was also deeply affectionate with his daughters from Khadijah, and especially his daughter Fatimah, wife of his cousin Ali, and their children.

Muhammad deeply loved his grandchildren on Khadijah's side, who were a constant reminder of his special relationship to her.

Khadijah was known to Muslims, as were Muhammad's other wives, "the Mother of the Faithful."

This is the word "Muhammad" in Arabic designed in a formative style which looks like a flower. Courtesy of artist Farid Al-Ali.

Muhammad and Polygamy

Muhammad did not introduce polygamy:

Men having more than one wife was common throughout history.[9] Jewish scripture speaks often of men with more than one wife, including Abraham, Jacob, and Solomon.

The Prophet was married to Khadijah for almost twenty-five years and with her fathered four girls and two boys. Both of his sons died in their childhood.

Married to One Wife for 25 Years

His life with Khadijah corresponded with the hardest days of his ministry, when he was reviled and rejected by the Quraysh and others. But after Khadijah's passing, the fortunes of Islam turned. Muhammad became the leader of a new community that had growing influence. He made treaties with other tribes. Also, in the battles between Muslims and their Meccan opponents, many Muslim men lost their lives, leaving many women widowed with fewer men available to marry.

Muhammad marries a Muslim widow: After Khadijah passed away, the Prophet married a poor widow, Sawdah. Her husband passed away after they returned from Abyssinia. His marriage to Sawdah was a form of support for her. Muhammad was nearly fifty-years-old when he married Sawdah, who was older than him.

Women

Muhammad marries the daughter of Abu-Bakr:
A few years later, Muhammad married Aisha, the
daughter of his dear friend and senior
consultant, Abu-Bakr. The marriage was an
honor for Abu-Bakr and Aisha.

**Muhammad marries the daughter
of Omar:** Two years later, Hafsa, the
daughter of another close companion, Omar, lost
her husband in the Battle of Uhud. Omar preferred
for Hafsa to marry one of his trusted friends, but she
did not receive a proposal. Muhammad, then, took
the initiative and proposed to her. The marriage was
an honor and support for Omar and his daughter.

**Muhammad marries a Muslim widow
and daughter of his enemy:** Ramlah
was the daughter of one of Muhammad's
leading Meccan adversaries, Abu-Sufyan.
Despite her father's hatred for Muhammad, Ramlah, also
known as Umm Habibah, embraced Islam and married a
Muslim. With her husband, she migrated to Abyssinia and
lived there for almost fifteen years. Her husband converted
to Christianity and passed away there. She was left alone
in Abyssinia, so Muhammad proposed to her and she
accepted. Surprisingly, her father embraced Islam one year
later.

Muhammad marries Safiyya, a woman from a Jewish tribe: The Bani-An-Nadhir was one of the Jewish tribes that betrayed Muhammad and worked against him. The Prophet besieged them in their city of Khaybar, and they surrendered. Safiyya, the daughter of their leader, was among those captured. Muhammad released her and proposed marriage to her. On several occasions, Safiyya described Muhammad as a loving and fair husband.

Mariya the Copt: Muhammad sent a messenger to the ruler of Egypt, who was Christian, calling him to accept the message of Islam. The ruler replied with a polite apology and sent the Prophet some gifts as well as a physician and a concubine named Mariya, or Mary. Muhammad accepted the gifts. He married Mariya and later on she gave birth to a baby boy named Ibrahim. Ibrahim died when he was a little boy, causing much grief for Muhammad and Mariya.

Muhammad conveyed God's command to control and limit polygamy: As was noted above, Muhammad often did not completely uproot customs of his time but created important changes for the better. A consistent theme of the Qur'an is social justice and the creation of a strong sense of human rights and responsibilities. The Qur'an created a stronger sense of individual rights, especially for women, and strengthened the family over the old tribal patterns of social organization.

Islam did not forbid polygamy but restricted and regulated it.

In Islam, it is not compulsory to marry more than one wife, but is permitted under certain conditions. The Qur'an makes a strong case for monogamy at the same time. In Surah 4:3 we read that a man should not marry more than one woman if he cannot treat them all with equal fairness and impartiality. Then later in the same surah at verse 129 we read:

> *"And it will not be within your power to treat your wives with equal fairness, however much you desire it."*

Many Muslims today argue that this provides a clear position by the Qur'an in preference of monogamy. Today the vast majority of Muslims around the world have monogamous marriages, with less than three percent of all Muslim marriages being polygamous.

Limits on the Prophet Muhammad: Some writers hostile to Islam have attacked Muhammad for having so many wives. First, it should be noted that Muhammad was married to more than four wives before he received the revelation of verses of Surah 4. But more importantly, his actions are not at all difficult to understand and were common within the arab society and for many world leaders throughout history.

The religious historian Geoffrey Parrinder remarks how few in history have been so maligned as Muhammad over the issue of plural wives:

"This man was not married until he was twenty-five years of age, then he and his wife lived in happiness and fidelity for twenty-four more years until her death when he was forty-nine. Only between the ages of fifty and his death at sixty-three did Muhammad take other wives, only one who was a virgin, and most of them were taken for dynastic and political reasons. Certainly the Prophet's record was better than the head of the Church of England, Henry VIII."[10]

Notes

1. Mustafa Akyol, *Islam without Extremes: A Muslim Case for Liberty* (New York: W.W. Norton, 2011), p. 54.

2. Narrated by Tirmidhii. According to other narrations prophet Muhammad indicated that whoever had one or two or three daughters and he properly looked after them (until they become independent) he would get into God's Paradise.

3. Karen Armstrong, *Muhammad: A Biography of the Prophet* (San Francisco: HarperSanFrancisco, 1992), p. 191.

4. Cited in *Sunan Abu-Dawud.*

5. The Qur'an emphasizes in many verses that a person must be good to both parents (e.g. Chapter 17:23).

6. See World Health Organization report, "Violence Against Women," November 2012 at http://www.who.int/mediacentre/factsheets/fs239/en/

7. Cited in *Tirmidhi.*

8. *Sahih Abu Dawood.* See also Qur'an 2: 229.

9. Regarding polygamy in other religions, earlier, there were no restrictions even in Hindu religion. It was only in 1954, when the Hindu Marriage Act was passed, that it became illegal for a Hindu to have more than one wife. At present, it is the Indian law that restricts a Hindu man from having more than one wife and not the Hindu scriptures.

10. Geoffrey Parrinder, *Mysticism in the World's Religions* (Oxford: One World, 1996), p. 121.

Chapter 7

Human Rights

"O mankind! We have created you from male and female, and have made you nations and tribes that you may know one another. The noblest of you, in the sight of God is the best in conduct. Verily! God is All-Knowing, All-Aware."

(Surah 49:13)

Human Rights
Freedom, Justice & Protection

"No compulsion" is an essential tenet of Islam:
Muhammad proclaimed himself as a Messenger of God. He received a divine message for humanity and struggled to convey it to all people, but he did not force any one to accept it. The Qur'an confirms the fundamental Islamic teaching in freedom of belief and freedom of choice for all people.

> *And if the Lord willed, all who are in the earth would have believed together. Would you [Muhammad] compel people until they are believers?*
> Surah 10:99
>
> *There is no compulsion in religion; truth stands out clear from error: whoever rejects evil and believes in God has grasped the most trustworthy hand-hold that never breaks.*
> *And God Hears and Knows all things.*
> Surah 2:256

Equality of all races:
In Islam, all people are considered equal under law by reason of their being members of the human race. Piety and excellent moral character are the only criteria for merit in the eyes of God. Muhammad put it in these words:

"Your Lord is One. All humankind are from Adam and Adam was created from dust. An Arab has no superiority over a non-Arab nor does a non-Arab have any superiority over an Arab except by piety." *Riyadh Al-Salihin.*

Slavery:

Slavery existed before Muhammad's time; it was part of many social systems in the world until the modern era. Slaves were considered as assets and part of people's wealth. Slaves were often considered less than human, inherently inferior to the ruling classes that enslaved men, women, and children.

Slavery is now formally outlawed but it still persists in the twenty-first century. It is estimated that over 27 million people around the world live in slavery today, and slavery in the form of sex trafficking of young girls is an international problem that is a shameful practice and sign of moral and spiritual decline.

Muhammad encouraged freeing slaves and introduced Islamic regulations to eliminate slavery: As we have seen, Muhammad was sensitive to any injustice and called for the strengthening of the rights of the weak in society: women, slaves, children, orphans. He did not abolish slavery, which was an entrenched part of Arab culture. But he made it clear that slaves were fully human and had rights and that they should be freed whenever possible to pursue their God-given talents as productive members of society. Muhammad encouraged Muslims to release slaves and the Qur'an specifically instructs Muslims against the sexual exploitation of slave girls:

> *"Force not your slave-girls to whoredom...that you may seek enjoyment of the life of the world."*
> Surah 24:33

All people stand on equal footing before the law: Muhammad emphasized that all people should respect the law and that offenders must be punished regardless of their social standing. When the law is applied justly, all people enjoy justice and security.

The Prophet made clear that no one is above the law, including his own relatives. He stated that he would punish his beloved daughter, Fatimah, if she stole from anyone.

The story of To'mah and a Jewish man: On one occasion, an Arab man, To'mah Ibn Ubayriq, stole a metal shield that was part of a suit of armor, and hid it in the home of his Jewish friend. The Jewish friend was accused of stealing the shield but denied the charge and testified under oath that To'mah was the thief.

As the facts were not yet clear, many Arab Muslims sympathized with To'mah and tried to influence Muhammad's opinion and to turn the case against the Jewish man. But Muhammad insisted on the protocols of Islamic justice. To'mah was proved guilty and the Jewish man was declared innocent. In this context, a Quranic verse was revealed to Muhammad asserting the primacy of justice:

> "Surely, We have revealed to you the Book with the truth, so that you may judge between people according to what God has shown you. Do not be an advocate for those who breach trust."
> Surah 4:105

Islamic calligraphy produced by the Turkish calligrapher Hassan Chelebi for a verse in the Qur'an. God says to people: "when you judge between people you judge with justice."
Surah 4:58

Women's rights and obligations:
Throughout Muhammad's ministry and through the revelations in the Qur'an, the rights of women were promoted. Muhammad reaffirmed protection of women's rights in his farewell address. He said:

> "O People, it is true that you have certain rights with regard to your women but they also have rights over you.

> "Remember that you have taken them as your wives only under God's trust and with His permission. Do treat your women well and be kind to them for they are your partners and committed helpers." *Riyadh Al-Salihin.*

Protection of orphans' rights:
Muhammad conveyed God's Commandments in relation to orphans. The Holy Qur'an commands Muslims to protect orphan's rights and to treat them with kindness and justice.

> "Lo! Those who devour the wealth of orphans wrongfully, they do but swallow fire into their bellies, and they will be exposed to burning flame."
> Surah 4:10

And Muhammad once said:

"I and the person who looks after an orphan, will be in Paradise like this"—putting his index and middle fingers together." *Tirmidhi*

Economic rights: As we have seen, Muhammad was concerned with teaching Muslims to follow the path of righteousness in all dealings, including in business and the handling of personal finances.

The Prophet was asked to lead a funeral prayer for a person, but he first asked his companions: "Did this man borrow money or have in his possessions any trusts that belong to others?" They replied, "Yes." So Muhammad then asked them to deliver the trusts to those entitled to them and then he would pray for the deceased.

"God commands you to restore deposits to their owners; and when you judge between people that you judge with justice. Verily, how excellent is the teaching that God gives you! Surely God is the All-Hearing, All-Seeing."
Surah 4:58

Muhammad indicated that on the Day of Judgment, God will be the foe for those who hire workers and don't pay them their wages. Prophet Muhammad emphasized that wages must be paid for workers before their sweat dries. Wages cannot be delayed and must be paid immediately after finishing work.

No usury in Islam: Muhammad was against any action that allowed the strong and powerful to dominate those who were in a weaker position. For this reason he was against the practice known in Arabic as riba. Riba literally means "increase, addition, expansion, or growth." In finance it is the practice of a lender receiving interest/usury (increase) when providing money to a borrower.

Is usury ethical?

This is, of course, an ancient practice and the religious prohibition of usury is very much a Judeo-Christian Islamic value. Here how it is referred to in Jewish scripture:

> "If you lend money to my people, to the poor among you, you shall not deal with them as a creditor; you shall not exact interest from them." (Exodus 22:25)

The sentiment here is that you should not reap what you do not sow and that taking interest is simply unfair. Muhammad once said: "God has forbidden you to take usury (*riba*), therefore all interest obligations shall henceforth be waived. Your capital is yours to keep. You will neither inflict nor suffer any inequity. God has judged that there shall be no riba (interest)."[4]

> *"Those who charge usury are in the same position as those controlled by the devil's influence. This is because they claim that usury is the same as trade. However, God permits trade and prohibits usury."*
> Surah 2:275

The Sanctity and Inviolability of Human Life

The Qur'an makes it clear that the first and most basic of human rights is the right to life. So sacred is this right in the Qur'an that the holy book of Islam claims that if someone commits murder it is as if he or she has killed all of humanity and if someone saves a life it is as if he or she has saved all of humanity.

Commenting on the biblical account of the first murder in history, when Cain, the son of Adam, killed his brother Abel, the Qur'an makes this uncompromising proclamation of human rights and a call to every person's conscience to protect this right to life:

> "Because of that [killing] we ordained for the Children of Israel that if anyone killed a person not in retaliation of murder, or to spread mischief in the land, it would be as if he killed all mankind, and if anyone saved a life, it would be as if he saved the life of all mankind."
> Surah 5:32

Muhammad considered committing suicide a major sin:

Muhammad put it in these words: "Whoever kills himself with a piece of metal, he will be resurrected on the Day of Judgment holding the same piece of metal and killing himself continuously in the hellfire forever; and whoever kills himself with a poison, he will be resurrected holding the same poison and swallowing it continuously in the hellfire forever; and whoever kills himself by throwing himself from a high place such as a mountain, he will do the same in the hellfire forever." *[this is for males and females]* *Sahih Al-Bukhari*

Honor killing and bloodshed forbidden: A sad fact across many cultures is the practice of honor killing: the murder of women or girls for suspected behavior that brings shame to a family's reputation. The honor killing of women cuts across religious traditions and is found even today among Muslims, Hindus, Christians, Jews, and Buddhists as well as among the nonreligious peoples. Indeed, domestic violence against women is a universal stain on contemporary society.

Muhammad also abolished the pre-Islamic Arab practice of vendetta and blood revenge. This was something deeply personal to the Prophet. His cousin Rabiah had been murdered by his Meccaan enemies during the early days of his ministry. According to the customs of his time, he could seek a bloody retaliation against his killers.

But in his farewell address Muhammad made a clean break with the past in favor of Islamic values, saying:

> "Revenge for blood shed as was the custom in the days of ignorance before Islam is forbidden. I forgive those who murdered my cousin, Rabiah."

Deliberate murder and killing by mistake: A deliberate murder is subject to retaliation in kind, the killer must be sentenced. But whoever kills someone by mistake or accidental death must pay compensation to the family of the deceased. At the time of Muhammad, the indemnity was one hundred camels.

Only fight those who fight you: Muslims have long been accused of spreading their religion through violence and war. This is not a fair accusation. We have seen how the early Muslims were forced to defend themselves against attacks from the Quraysh-led opposition. Muhammad taught his followers to be assertive with their enemies, neither submissive nor aggressive. He was inevitably involved in battles, and he set clear rules and ethics of engagement with enemies in battle and compassionate rules for dealing with prisoners of war that were far more humane than anything known until modern times.

This is the word "Muhammad" in Arabic being designed in a formative style. Courtesy of artist Farid Al-Ali.

Muhammad taught Muslims not to fight civilians and not to attack or kill children, women, or elders. He asked them not to destroy the environment or damage trees. He always reminded them that the involvement in battles should be for the sake of God Who does not like transgressors or oppressors. The Qur'an makes this clear:

DO NOT KILL
civilians, children, women and elders,

DO NOT DESTROY
environment and do not cut trees

"And fight for the sake of God those who fight you and don't transgress the limits. Verily, God does not like transgressors."
Surah 2:190

Muhammad condemned violence: Muhammad never used violence as a tool to convey God's message or impose God's religion. He taught believers that whenever and wherever gentleness or kindness is used, it will bring about good results. He also taught that roughness and rudeness in behavior will spoil every affair.

Note

For a comprehensive discussion of Islamic financial teachings, see M. Yaqub Mirza, *Five Pillars of Prosperity: Essential of Faith-Based Wealth Building* (Ashland, OR: White Cloud Press, 2014).

Chapter 8

Environment

The bowing tree was found in a camping site in Nowra, south of Sydney, Australia. It resembles bowing to God in the Muslim's prayers. The lower edge of the tree looks like the head of a bowing person.

Muhammad's Teachings to Preserve the Environment

Muhammad called for a green world:

The Prophet of Islam linked the preservation of the environment to belief in God who created all beings. Therefore, a believer in God must not cause harm to the environment because it is part of God's kingdom. Harming the environment and wasting or polluting its resources (water, plants, animals, soil, air, marine ecosystem, etc.) is not acceptable from an Islamic point of view.

"Any Muslim who plants a seed that grows to a level, people or animals or birds can benefit from it, then this act is considered *sadaqa* [a charity that is rewarded by God]."

Saying of Muhammad ﷺ

Natural resources are in perfect equilibrium:
Muhammad taught that all natural resources were created by God and were set in perfect equilibrium.

> *"Verily all things We created are in proportion and measure."*
> Surah 54:49
>
> *"... and everything with Him is in due proportion."*
> Surah 13:8
>
> *"...such is the artistry of Allah, who disposes of all things in perfect order."*
> Surah 27:88

People have equal rights to natural resources: Natural resources are the gift of God to all mankind. They should not be wasted or monopolized. Muhammad stated that people have equal rights to water, grass, and energy.

Live Green

Don't pollute the environment

Don't damage the environment

Don't waste/overuse natural resources

Use natural resources efficiently, consider recycling

Fauna and flora are the creation of God
"Blessed be Allah, the best of creators"

Surah 23:14

"No harm" is the general rule of life: Muhammad set a general rule for protecting natural resources, preserving the environment, and securing people when he said to his companions, "You are not to harm or to be harmed."

"Faith can be branched into more than seventy parts, topped by testifying the oneness of God. The last part is removing harm from people's way."

Saying of Muhammad ﷺ

This is the word "Muhammad" written in a formative style of Arabic calligraphy. It looks like green leaves from a tree.

Muhammad emphasized water rationing and condemned wasting and overuse:

The Prophet stated clearly to a companion who was performing ablutions before prayer not to waste water, even if he were close to a running river. On another occasion Muhammad told his companions not to pollute stagnant water or urinate in it.

God says in the Qur'an:

"...Out of water, We made every living creature."

"Verily the wasteful people are the brothers of devils and the Satan has ever been ungrateful to his Lord."

"waste not by excess, for God loveth not the wasters."
Surahs 21:30; 17:27; 7:31

Protect the environment no matter what: Muhammad encouraged people to continuously work to safeguard our environment, even if the world is coming to an end. He said:

"If the Hour [the end of worldly life] came and someone had a seedling in his hand and he were able to plant it, then let him do it."

Believers in God are required to preserve and protect the environment. God does not like those who cause corruption on earth by destroying it.

Protect the Earth

> "... do good, as God has been good to thee. And seek not to work corruption in the earth; surely God loves not the workers of corruption."
> Surah 28:77

Animals and all creatures form part of a greater community of life on Earth:

"There is not an animal or creature that lives and moves on the earth, nor a being that flies on its wings, but they are communities like you. We have not neglected anything in the Book and they [all creation] shall be gathered to their Lord in the end."

Surah 6:38

Muhammad called for the ethical treatment of animals:

The Prophet was against detaining or confining or restraining animals for no genuine reason. Also, he didn't like lashing animals or hitting them. He used different teaching styles to emphasize the spiritual call to treat animals with care and dignity.

Halal Meat

Halal **means more than** *halal* **food:** *Halal* is most commonly used to define permissable foods, but the term is much broader. *Halal* means "permissable" foods *or* actions, and is the opposite of *haram*, unlawful acts. Muhammad taught that Muslims have no right to kill any animal unless permitted by God. It is only with God's permission (to whom all creatures belong) that certain types of animals can be slaughtered for human consumption. Only vegetarian animals can be slaughtered to be eaten with the exception of pigs (e.g., cows, sheep, chicken, and birds that eat no flesh).

Muhammad taught his followers that lawful killing of animals should be done in the least painful manner: For example, the animal cannot be killed by a blunt blade (it must be sharp). An animal must not be hit by a stone or slaughtered next to another animal watching the slaughtering process. Muhammad said to a person who was slaughtering an animal beside another one: **"Do you want to kill the other animal twice?"**

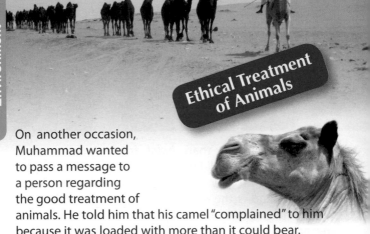

Ethical Treatment of Animals

On another occasion, Muhammad wanted to pass a message to a person regarding the good treatment of animals. He told him that his camel "complained" to him because it was loaded with more than it could bear.

And he even once told his companions, "Whoever captured the babies of this bird should return them back to their mother."

You will be rewarded for being kind to animals:

A kind act, even to animals, deserves to be rewarded by God. Muhammad once told his companions the story of a thirsty man who found a well of water and went down to drink. When he went up, he found a dog gasping in thirst, so the man went down in the well again to fill his shoe with water and brought it up to the dog. God was thankful for this man's compassion and forgave his past sins.

On another occasion Muhammad told his companions that God had punished a woman because she imprisoned and confined a cat until it died. She neither fed the cat nor let it go.

Environment

Chapter 9

The Miracle

"Or do they say, 'Why, he has forged it?'
Say: 'Then produce a sura like it, and
call on whom you can, apart from God,
if you speak truly.'
Surah 10:38

"What, do they not ponder the Quran?
If it had been from other than God
surely they would have found in it
much inconsistency."
Surah 4:82

God's Miracle to Muhammad

Muhammad is beloved by Muslims because he demonstrated throughout his life the very best of human qualities. The Prophet Muhammad is not a regarded as a divine person—"fully God and fully man"—as in some Christian interpretations of Jesus. Muhammad is a man who was inspired at special times in his life by the Angel Gabriel, the Angel of Revelation. Muhammad displayed the best of human qualities in the midst of a ministry filled with personal attacks on him, his family, and followers. Muslims revere Muhammad because of the qualities he exhibited throughout his life but also because he was the bearer of God's words as found in the Qur'an.

One way to think about this in comparison to Christianity is not to equate Muhammad with Jesus and then equate the New Testament with the Qur'an. Rather, for Christians, Jesus is the Word of God and the means of salvation, while in Islam the Qur'an is the  Word of God and means of salvation. The New Testament, then, is more like the record of hadiths in Islam which provide us with a narrative of the life and times of Muhammad just as the New Testament provides us with stories relating to the life and times of Jesus.

Although his life is filled with amazing feats that many Muslims deem as showing God's favor and grace toward him (what some would call miraculous interventions), Muhammad made it clear that the only true miracle of his ministry is the text of the Qur'an, the inspired revelations  that came through him but were not his words. The Qur'an is a message of mercy and compassion from God.

Unlike physical miracles mentioned in other scriptures (feeding of masses, raising the dead), Muslims feel that such miracle stories are only meaningful to one who was present at the time they occurred. But the Qur'an is always available for the believer to access and find support for his or her spiritual life.

The words of the Qur'an address great spiritual truths as well as practical morals. The Qur'an boldly claims that

 God is unseen to eyes but is known through the stirrings of the soul, through holy books, and in all of creation. For Muslims, all the world becomes a landscape of divine disclosure.

> *"And to God belongs the East and the West. So wherever you turn to, then, again, there is the countenance of God. Truly, God is the One who is infinite, all-knowing."*
>
> Surah 2:115

The authenticity of the Qur'an text: The question of accuracy and authenticity of holy scriptures is a hot topic in religious studies. Scholars of all faiths naturally spend a great amount of effort to understand the history of their scriptures, which have their origins in ancient history. Biblical scholarship has taken us a long way toward a better understanding the formation of the Hebrew and Christian scriptures through what is known as "source critical studies" of the text.

Scholars of the Qur'an (Muslim and non-Muslim) generally agree that with the Qur'an we are on firmer ground than with older scriptures. There is a general consensus that the Qur'an we have is the authentic revelations that came to Muhammad during moments of revelation. There is a strong record within Islamic history of how important the Qur'an was during the lifetime of Muhammad. Many of his companions memorized the entire Qur'an and recited it precisely with the approval of Muhammad.

This is part of a verse in the Qur'an. God says to His people: "Call Me and I will answer you." Surah 40:60

As the Qur'an is by its very name a recitation of the words of God, the act of reciting the Qur'an in beautiful chant form became one of the first great religious acts of the early Islamic community.

> *"So when the Qur'an is recited, listen to it and keep silent."*
> **Surah 7:204**
>
> *"...and recite the Qur'an in slow, measured rhythmic tones."*
> **Surah 73:4**

Soon after the passing of Muhammad, the complete Qur'an was compiled into one book. One of the causes for creating this written compilation was a threat of schism in the early Muslim community.

After the Prophet's death there was a great upheaval in Arabia that led to what are known as the Ridda (or Apostate), when some tribes that had pledged loyalty to Muhammad and Islam broke their treaties with the Muslims, now led by the Caliph Abu Bakr.

In the Battle of Yamama some 70 Muslims who had memorized the entire Qur'an were killed. This was a potentially dire threat to the preservation of the Qur'anic text. There was a fear that with this loss of Quranic reciters parts of the sacred book might become lost to the Muslims. Under the leadership of the first caliphs, care was taken to protect the Qur'an by writing it down and creating a unified text.

Distinctiveness of the Qur'an: As we have seen, the sayings of Muhammad and his lessons to early followers were not mixed with the Qur'an revelations. Muhammad's sayings and teachings are collected in books that are called "The Sunnah or Hadith of the Prophet." They include his teachings, stories of how he conducted his life, and explanations of the Qur'an. The Qur'an is always the preeminent focus of Islamic life, with the Prophet the beloved hero and archetype of the perfect human being.*

Reciting the Qur'an: Anyone who has heard the Muslim call to prayer has some sense of the power of Arabic as a sacred language. Still more powerful are the very words of the Qur'an in Arabic. As we have emphasized, the Qur'an is meant to be put into the lives of believers through its recitation. The rhyming prose of the Arabic text produces profound impact on those who recite or hear the Qur'an.

Tajweed
Rules for recitation of the Qur'an

There are strict rules for recitation of the Qur'an that go all the way back to Muhammad's day. Muslims trust it is not only the Qur'anic text that was uniquely preserved but also the styles in which Muhammad and his companions recited it.

The styles of reciting the Qur'an are documented by its narrators and reciters starting from those who heard it from Muhammad. This chain of recitation runs across the whole Islamic world—from one generation to another, from Muhammad until today.

* See Chapter 10 on the Wisdom of Muhammad as found in his sayings.

The richness of the Arabic language: Linguists agree with Muslims that Arabic is an incredibly rich language. Arabic is a verbal language, with words generally derived from three letter root words; for example, k-t-b (*kataba*) is the verb "to write." From this verb root a whole range of words follow: book = *kitáb*; writer = *kátib*; written = *maktúb*; library = *maktaba*; correspondence = *mokátaba*; bookseller = *kutbiy*; reporter = *mokáteb* , and so on.

To the native speaker, these variations from the root verb create a rich tapestry of meanings; and for those learning Arabic it creates a web of references that makes learning the language very intuitive if daunting due to the millions of words generated by these patterns and forms. Joel Carmichael in his book *The Shaping of the Arabs* writes how this richness of Arabic means that "Arabic loses on translation but all other languages gain on being translated into Arabic."

Muslims take tremendous pride in learning Arabic and being able to recite the Qur'an in its original form. And this is why translations are never referred to as the text of the Qur'an. Only the Arabic text is the Holy Qur'an and all translations are really commentaries that help non-Arabic speakers gain a sense of appreciation of the contents of this holy scripture.

What is considered the true miracle of the Qur'an is how it shaped Islamic culture and thought and became the foundation for one of the greatest revolutions in religious history. Following the death of Muhammad in 632 CE, the Muslim world, guided by the Qur'an, erupted out of the Arabian Peninsula and in 125 years Muslims came to rule from Spain to India.

More than this, Muslims guided by the Qur'an established a Pax Islamica in which religious minorities were generally protected and given rights, trade was expanded, scientific research and technology was advanced, and literature and the arts flowered. Jews, Christians, Zoroastrians, and other non-Muslims were key players in this ecumenical movement that created the world's most sophisticated civilization that eventually ruled from Europe to the Far East.

This is all part of the great miracle of the Qur'an.

The Qur'an is commonly printed in 604 pages. It contains approximately 80,000 words, which form 6348 verses that comprise 114 chapters. The longest chapter in the Holy Qur'an is composed of 286 verses and the shortest one is composed of three verses only.

Qur'an and Science

Muslims were motivated by their faith to seek knowledge from the cradle to the grave, and to go in quest of knowledge even unto China. This led to a great flourishing of scientific research and development within the Muslim world. Under Muslim leadership, Muslims, Christians, Greeks, Jews, and Zoroastrians translated Greek and Persian philosophical and scientific texts into the new international language of Arabic.

Muslim philosopher-scientists (in Islam nearly all scientists were also philosophers), studied and wrote on religious thought, economics, astronomy, mathematics, medicine, botany, zoology, embryology, meteorology, and so on.

Today, many Muslims turn to the Qur'an and see in certain verses hints of modern scientific findings.

> *We will show them Our signs in the horizons and within themselves until it becomes clear to them that it is the truth.*
> Surah 41:53
> *Say (unto them, O Muhammad): Are those who know equal with those who know not?*
> Surah 39:9

The big bang and the creation of the universe:

In Muhammad's day, ideas of the formation of the universe and the motion of the planets and stars was minimal and based on limited information. Fourteen centuries ago, the Qur'an refers to the origins of the universe, the motion of the sun and the moon, and the rotation of the earth in ways that suggest parallels to modern scientific views.

Our current scientific understanding of the origins of the universe is known as the Big Bang Theory, which is supported by observational and experimental data gathered over decades. According to the Big Bang Theory the whole universe was initially one extremely dense mass that nearly 14 billion years ago began to rapidly expan, this rapid expansion being the big bang! This led to the formation of galaxies out of agglomerated clouds of celestial matter in a gaseous form.[3]

The expansion of the universe:

In 1925, American astronomer Edwin Hubble provide observational evidence that stars are moving away from each other, which implies that galaxies and the whole universe is expanding. Also, today we know that planets move in elliptical orbits around the sun and rotate around their axes. In the poetic imagery of the Qur'an, Muhammad recited these prescient verses:

"Do not the Unbelievers see that the heavens and the earth were joined together [as one unit of creation], before we clove them asunder? We made from water every living thing. Will they not then believe?"

Surah 21:30

He, [God] turned to the heaven when it was smoke and said to it and to the earth: come together willingly or unwillingly, they said: we come together in willing obedience."

Surah 41:11

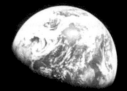

"And it is He Who created the night and the day, and the sun and the moon. All [the celestial bodies] swim along, each in its rounded course."

Surah 21:33

"With power and skill We created the heaven and We are continuously expanding it."

Surah 51:47

Embryology: Muhammad recited the following verse that describes the formation of the fetus. Such knowledge was not known in Muhammad's time.

> *"He created you in the wombs of your mothers, creation after creation, in a threefold gloom. Such is God, your Lord. His is the Sovereignty. There is no God save Him. How then are ye turned away?*
> Surah 39:6

Modern science explains that there are three layers that form veils of darkness that surround the fetus in the womb and provide sturdy and powerful protection for the embryo; (1) the interior abdominal wall of the mother, (2) the uterine wall and (3) the amino-chorionic membrane.

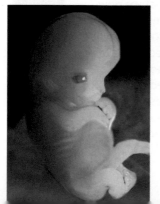

The creation of the fetus is described in the Qur'an in a fashion that is far ahead of its time:

sperm

"Verily We created man from a product of wet earth. Then placed him as a drop (of seed) in a safe lodging. Then We made the sperm into a clot of congealed blood; then of that clot We made a lump; then we made out of that lump bones and clothed the bones with flesh; then we developed out of it another creation."
Surah 23:12-14

blood clot

This Quranic description of the development of the embryo is identical to what we now understand as fact. Also, once research methods became possible for such study, we

fetus lump

learned for certain that bones were formed before the flesh, exactly as mentioned in this verse from the Qur'an.[4]

bones

flesh

Furthermore, scientists have discovered that the hearing sense for the embryo develops in the mother's womb before the sense of sight. This is compatible with the sequence mentioned in the Qur'an—verses 32:9, 76:2, and 23:78 all refer to the hearing sense before sight.

> *"...So blessed be Allah the best of Creators."*
> *Surah 23:14*

Notes

1. Joel Carmichael, *The Shaping of the Arabs: A Study of Ethnic Identity* (New York: Macmillan, 1967)

2. On Muslim civilization, see Marshal G. S. Hodgson, *The Venture of Islam*, 3 vols. (Chicago: University of Chicago Press, 1974.)

3. Tibi Puiu, "Elemental Gas Clouds Formed Minutes After the Big Bang Found" at http://www.zmescience.com/space/elemental-gas-clouds-formed-minutes-after-the-big-bang-found/#EMTo4Is5BKCfow9I.99).

4. See more information about embryology at: www.quranandscience.com; www.islamreligion.com; www.islamhouse.com

Chapter 10

His Sayings

Muhammad said while interlacing the fingers of his two hands:

"Believers are like a structure, they support each other."
(Bukhari)

Muhammad's sayings and teachings are highly influential as they cover most aspects of life: spirituality, morals, marriage and family life, commerce, and more. These sayings of Muhammad emanate from a base of wisdom and divine revelation.

Muhammad's sayings, actions, and attributes are known as *sunnah* (custom) and are embodied in collections of sayings, or hadith. The sunnah represents the second source of Islamic legislation after the Qur'an.

"Your companion [Muhammad] has not strayed from the path of truth nor has he been deluded. Nor does he speak out of whim."
Surah 53:2-3

Hope

Fated Death

Mankind

Muhammad drew three lines on the sand and said: "This is the human being (who has many hopes and plans in this worldly life). While he lives to attain or accomplish these hopes, death comes to him."
(Bukhari)

"Worship God as if you see Him, for if you do not see Him, He sees you."
(Bukhari)

"Avail five before five: Your youth before old age, fitness before sickness, wealth before poverty, free time before busy time, and life before death."
(Riyadh al-Salaheen)

"The most perfect of the faithful in religion is the most beautiful of them in character."
(Tirmidhi)

"In you are two qualities which God and
His Messenger love: deliberation and forbearance."
(Tirmidhi)

"The search for knowledge is incumbent
upon every Muslim."
(Ibn Maja)

"Two graces, many people underestimate:
health and leisure time."
(Riyadh al-Salaheen)

"Make things easy to people (concerning religious
matters), and do not make it hard for them; give them
good tidings and do not make them run away."
(Bukhari)

"Those who do honest trading and business based on clear
terms, God blesses them and their business (trade). Contrary,
God does not bless those who lie and hide facts."
(Bukhari)

"One of the beauties of a man's Islam is that
he refrains from that which is not his concern."
(Tirmidhi)

"You will not be a believer in God unless you like for your brethren what you like for yourself."
(Bukhari)

"Every Muslim should pay sadaqah *(charitable contributions). If he does not have sufficient funds, then let him work in order to benefit himself and be able to pay charity. If he does not have a job, then let him help others (this is an act of charity). If he doesn't find anyone to help, let him do good deeds and refrain from doing bad or evil deeds. This is a charity for him."*
(Bukhari)

"When man dies, he gains no rewards except from three things: in case he had dedicated a charity that people can continuously profit from; or he had left knowledge or a science that benefits the humanity; or if he had left a good (faithful) son who keeps on praying and asking God's blessings and forgiveness to his parents."
(Tirmidhi)

"Fear God wherever you are; follow a bad deed with a good deed as it erases it; and deal with people with high ethics."
(Tirmidhi)

"Goodness [rightness] is good morality;
and sin [misdeed]is what embarrasses you,
and you hate it to be known by others."
(Muslim

"A strong person is not the one who throws his
adversaries to the ground. A strong person is he who
contains himself when he is angry."
(Bukhari)

"Whoever believes in Allah and the Day of Judgment
should say good (words) or keep silent; and who ever
believes in Allah and the Day of Judgment must honor
(be generous with) his neighbor; and whoever believes in
Allah and the Day of Judgment must honor (be generous
with) his guest."
(Muslim)

(All of the above sayings are applicable for both males and females.)

Muhammad's Sayings on Diet and Health

> *"Eat and drink the sustenance God has provided and do not act wrongfully on earth."*
> *Surah 2:60*

Prevention is better than a cure:

Although Muhammad was not a physician, we have many sayings in the collections of hadith that relate to food, healthy eating habits, treatment with herbs, and what we today refer to as "alternative medicine." These sayings have been collected in books on "The Prophetic Medicine."[1]

Accounts of Muhammad's life highlight how he lived simply and moderately in all things, including his diet. The Prophet encouraged Muslims to not over indulge or do things in excess. In terms of diet and health, this meant first off not overeating. Muhammad indicated on many occasions that small meals were preferable and that we should not fill the stomach.

Don't Overeat!

It is part of Muhammad's teachings to have small meals during the day. He recommends keeping the stomach no more than two-thirds full. Portion control in diet is now understood to have great health benefits. By not over eating to the point of a full stomach, proper digestion occurs and the body does not have to work so hard.

Overeating also causes an unhealthy increase in glucose levels. Eating smaller portions helps keeps one's blood sugar regulated and stable. Portion control in eating helps maintain a healthy weight. In our contemporary culture, obesity and diabetes are pandemic. Following Muhammad's simple guidance can help create a healthy population.

Muhammad prescribing barley: Specific foods were recommended by Muhammad. Today, there is a great deal of research that demonstrates the great health benefits of barley.

Barley is a whole food supplement. It contains a wide spectrum of enzymes, vitamins, minerals, phytochemicals and all eight essential amino acids including tryptophan, which helps prevent depression.

Muhammad recommended barley soup (*talbina*) for stomach disorders and indicated that it helps relieve sorrow and depression. His wife Aisha used to recommend the close relatives of a deceased person to have *talbina* soup in order to relieve sorrow.

According to medical research, depression is found to be caused by a decrease of certain chemicals or neurotransmitters in the brain that are responsible for mood. Antidepressants stimulate chemical changes that increase the levels of these neurotransmitters.

It is revealing that Muhammad did not indulge in regular consumption of wheat bread, but mostly ate barley and bread made from barley flour. Today, we know that whole grain barley has many health benefits: It can regulate blood sugar, prevent tiny blood clots, and reduce the body's production of cholesterol.

The three main neurotransmitters associated with mood are serotonin, norepinephrine, and dopamine. Barley contains serotonin and medical studies have shown how adding barley to one's diet can have a positive impact on depression. Muhammad's prescription of barley 1400 years ago for relief of depression is a striking example of prophetic wisdom.

Zamzam mineral water: Zamzam is the name of mineral water that comes out of a well 20 meters east of Ka'bah in the sacred city of Mecca. Muslims believe it was miraculously generated thousands of years ago when Ibrahim's son Ishmael was thirsty and kept crying and kicking the ground until water gushed out (after his mother Hagar spent a lot of time looking for water).

Zamzam water is slightly alkaline (pH=7.5), and has a distinct taste. (Please note that drinking demineralized water such as distilled waters will create an acid pH in the stomach and intestines. Also, it will aggravate acid reflux).

Muhammad said that Zamzam water is blessed water from God. It is a lavish meal and a healer from many diseases.

Mineral water is classified by the U.S. Food and Drug Authority as having at least 250 parts per million (ppm) of total dissolved solids (TDS).

Chemical analysis of Zamzam water revealed that it has an average of 1000 ppm of mg/L, TDS. However, it complies with World Health Organization standards for potable water.

This special water is nearly a plentiful meal in itself, containing a range of minerals that the body needs such as calcium for strong bones and for the heart, muscles, and nerves to function properly, fluoride for healthy teeth, and bicarbonates for digestion.

Medicinal Truffles:

> Muhammad said: "Truffles are a kind of manna sent down upon the children of Israel, and their juice is a medicine for the eyes."[2]

Truffles are a fleshy fungus mushroom-like plant that belongs to the Agaricaceaa family. It grows in groups under the surface of the soil (2-50 cm deep) in moist desert areas without roots.

Analysis of truffles shows that they are 77% water and the remaining part is a mix of protein, fat, carbohydrates, and other materials. However, modern science discoveries indicate that the liquid of truffles has an effective curative effect for many eye disorders, including trachoma, an infectious eye disease that causes damage to the cornea cells.

Muhammad on olive oil:

In the Qur'an there is a description of the olive tree as being especially blessed.

"God is the Light of the heavens and the earth. The similitude of His light is as a niche wherein is a lamp. The lamp is in a glass. The glass is as it were a shining star. This lamp is kindled from a blessed tree, an olive neither of the East nor of the West, whose oil would almost glow forth (of itself) though no fire touched it. Light upon light. God guides unto His light whom He will. And God speaks to mankind in allegories, for God is Knower of all things."
Surah 24:35

The Prophet recommended to his companions to eat olive oil and to anoint their bodies with it. All modern scientific research confirms that olive oil is full of health benefits. Most of the fatty acid "building blocks" that make up olive oil come from monosaturated fat (good fat), which offers protection against heart disease by controlling LDL (bad cholesterol) while elevating HDL (good cholesterol) levels.

Olive oil is easy on the stomach. Its protective function aids in the treatment of ulcers and gastritis. Extra virgin olive oil, from the first pressing of the olives, contains higher levels of antioxidants, particularly vitamin E and phenols, because it is less processed. Today, olive oil is considered a good remedy for skin problems and an effective moisturizer.

Those at risk of diabetes are advised to combine a low-fat/high carbohydrate diet with olive oil. Studies show this combination is superior at controlling blood sugars levels compared to a diet that consists entirely of low-fat meals.

Notes

1. For an overview of Islamic teachings on health and medicine, see Fazlur Rahman, *Health and Medicine in the Islamic Tradition* (Chicago: Kazi Publications, 1997).
2. Narrated by Bukhari, Muslim, and Tirmidhi.

Chapter 11

Epilogue

The Prophet Muhammad Mosque
(Al-Masjid Al-Nabawi) Medina,
Saudi Arabia

Note: The house and the tomb of Muhammad
were joined to the mosque.

Muhammad and the Key to the Ka'bah

Islam, as a vibrant and living faith tradition, looks back to the life of Muhammad and his prophetic wisdom, and Muslims strive to make those teachings alive in today's twenty-first century world. We close these reflections on Muhammad's life and teachings with a story that shows the continuity of tradition from Muhammad's day to our time.

In the year 630 CE, Muhammad victoriously entered Mecca and defeated his long-time adversaries, the Quraysh leaders of the sacred city. He did not make Mecca his home, but rather came to liberate the Ka'bah from Quraysh control and to end the practice of idol worship. He came to liberate the Ka'bah and restore it to its original purpose. The Ka'bah was established by the prophet Abraham for the worship of one God.

Muhammad triumphantly entered the sacred sanctuary and called for the key to the door of the Ka'bah. The keeper of the key was a man named Uthman bin Talha of the Bani-Shaybah family. This family had been custodians of the Ka'bah since before Muhammad's time. This honor was passed from father to son.

Uthman bin Talha was a new Muslim. Early in Muhammad's ministry, he had refused Muhammad access to the Ka'bah for prayer. Now that Muhammad was returning as the new ruler of Mecca, Uthman had no choice but to give Muhammad the key, expecting to lose the honor of custodian of the shrine.

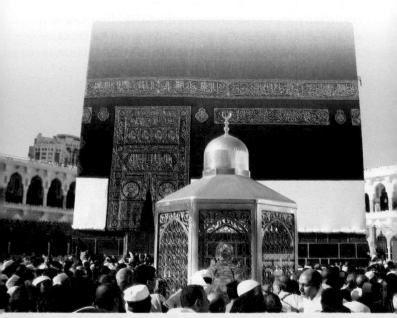

Many of Muhammad's companions felt they might be the new custodian and pressed upon Muhammad their request to hold this honor. Muhammad remained silent for several minutes, then took the key from Uthman, opened the Ka'bah door, and cleared the interior sanctuary of all idols. He next turned to Uthman bin Talha and said to him:

"Today is the day of loyalty and piety! Take the key back. As from now until the Day of Judgment, no on can take it from you [the Bani-Shayba family] unless he is an aggressor."

And then the Prophet asked his companion Bilal to climb on the top of the Ka'bah and call:

"God is greatest! God is greatest! I witness that there is no god but Allah, and I witness that Muhammad is His messenger!"

A moment of fidelity that has lasted until today: From that day to today, through all the changes of fortunes and kingdoms, the Bani-Shayba family has held its position. More than 1400 years have passed and the key is still given from one generation of the Bani-Shayba family to the next.

Today, when the Saudi authorities perform the annual cleaning and preparation of the Ka'bah for the annual pilgrimage, they contact the Bani-Shayba custodian of the Ka'bah to open the sanctuary.

This is one symbolic way in which the figure of Muhammad remains alive in the hearts of millions in our times. Karen Armstrong, author of *Muhammad: A Prophet for Our Time*, suggests that all people, Muslims and non-Muslims, approach the life of Muhammad in a balanced way in order to appreciate his achievements. He bears important lessons for all of us, not just for Muslims.

Muhammad literally suffered blood, sweat, and tears to bring peace to a war-torn Arabia of his day. His life was a tireless campaign against greed, injustice, and arrogance. The Christian scholar of Islam, W. Montgomrery Watt gave us this assessment of the life and mission of Muhammad:

"The more one reflects on the history of Muhammad and of early Islam, the more one is amazed at the vastness of his achievement. Circumstances presented him with an opportunity such as few men have had, but the man was fully matched with the hour."[1]

Notes

1. W. Montgomery Watt, *Muhammad at Medina* (Oxford: Oxford Unversity Press, 1962) p. 335.

Chapter 12

Islamic Art, Calligraphy
And Architecture

Photo taken by Peter Gould. Sultan Qaboos Grand Mosque - Oman

Islamic art and calligraphy, Bahrain ▲

Digital Artist Peter Gould

Sydney-born designer and digital artist Peter Gould founded Azaan
(www.azaan.com.au) to explore his passion for contemporary
graphic design, art, photography, and the rich visual & spiritual
traditions of Islam. His travels and studies throughout the Muslim
world have inspired a unique cultural fusion that is reactive
to a world of misunderstanding. Peter's work has reached
many audiences locally and abroad through exhibitions and
collaborations with other artists.

Peter Sanders, UK

Peter Sanders is a British photographer who started his career in the mid 1960s. He built up a photographic archive of more than a quarter

million photographs from all over the world. His first book *In the Shade of the Tree* gives a wonderful insight into the diversity of the Muslim cultures around the world. Sanders was selected by the Moroccan government to photograph and document the most important mosques and Islamic architecture in Morocco.

Hassan Çelebi, Turkey

Hassan Çelebi is one of the most famous Islamic calligraphers in the world. Since he began teaching Islamic calligraphy in 1976, Çelebi has issued over forty "ijazah" (diploma in Islamic calligraphy) to students from all over the world. He produced unique calligraphy pieces for renowned Islamic historical places and mosques, including: the Prophet Muhammad's Mosque and Quba Mosque in Medina, Saudi Arabia; the Mosque in Istanbul, Turkey; Fatih Mosque in Pfortzheim, Germany; Jum'ah Mosque in Johannesburg, South Africa; Almati Jum'ah Mosque in Kazakhstan; and the Islamic Medical Centre in Kuwait.

Mohamed Zakariya, USA

Zakariya is an American calligrapher who is considered the preeminent ambassador of the art of Islamic calligraphy in America. He learned Arabic and Islamic calligraphy when he was 19 in Morocco, Spain, and England. He is the first American to earn two licenses in Islamic calligraphy from Turkey. He is also known for his design of the "Eid Greetings" on the U.S. postage stamp ("Eid" means feast). He concentrates primarily on classical Arabic and Ottoman Turkish calligraphy.

 This calligraphy is a presentation for the verse:
"Is the reward for good [anything] but good?" Sura 55:60

Nuria Garcia Masip, Spain

Nuria Garcia Masp is a professional calligrapher from Ibiza, Spain. After receiving her degree from the George Washington University, she studied Islamic arts in Morocco then moved to Istanbul where she received her diploma in Islamic calligraphy in 2007. She currently pursues her calligraphic career through exhibitions, competitions, and workshops, moving between the United States, Morocco, Turkey, Europe, South Africa, and the Middle East. Her works revive classical texts through aesthetically arresting presentation.

200

Salva Rasool, India

Ms. Rasool holds a degree of applied art from the Sir J.J. School or Art in Mumbai. She incorporates an element of harmony in each genre she creates by keeping the balance between the original Arabic text and her modern contemporary artwork. She is known for creatively incorporating unconventional materials like terracotta, ceramics, pottery, glass and leather in her works.

In the name of Allah, the Gracious, the Merciful

This piece shows the first chapter of the Qur'an that Muslims recite in their daily prayers. It is called, "Al-Fatiha" or "The Opening."

Celina Cebula, Poland

Celina Cebula graduated from Pedagogical University in Cracow, Poland. and specialized in decorative art and artistic education. With her distinctive talent to mix calligraphy with painting she was able to reflect new meanings in her artistic designs.

The word Muhammad, the Messenger of God in Arabic mirrored over a colorful background ▶

"Unless you show mercy to others, Allah will not be merciful to you".

"Who does not thank people does not thank God".

Haji Noor Deen, China

Born in 1963 in Shangdong province, China, Noor Deen is one of the most renowned calligraphers, creating a unique link between Chinese and Arabic calligraphy.

The artistic pieces indicate: "There is no God but Allah, Muhammad is the Messenger of Allah". The dome in the bottom part is formed from the statement "Muhammad is the Messenger of Allah"

Nobuko Sagawa, Japan

Nobuko Sagawa is one of the most celebrated Japanese masters of Arabic calligraphy. She studied fine arts in Japan and became interested in the Arabic arts and letters. Mrs. Sagawa developed a style of "collaboration" among combinations of Japanese scripts (kana), Chinese characters (kanji), and Arabic letters. Her talent in mastering the "Thuluth" and "Kufi" Arabic fonts enabled her to generate creative calligraphic designs.

"And We have not sent you but to all people as a bearer of glad tidings and as a warner."

Sura 34:28

204

Farid Al-Ali, Kuwait

Al-Ali is the director of the Kuwait Center of Islamic Art and is one of the most acclaimed artists in the Middle East. He is known for his resourceful designs and inventive art. In 2005 he released "Muhammadeyat", a collection of 500 artwork designs generated from the word "Muhammad" in Arabic (please see below). The 500 designs are split into 11 groups (soft, square, hexagonal, octagonal, etc). Moreover, Al-Ali did a similar collection to "Muhammadeyat", but derived from the word "Allah."

Mohammed Mandi, U.A.E.

With his unique experience and creative designs, Mohammed Mandi was nominated to design the Arabic calligraphy on the banknote and passports of U.A.E. and many other countries. In addition, he was nominated to supervise calligraphic designs in Shaikh Zayed Grand Mosque in Abu Dhabi, U.A.E. and many other mosques in the world.

An artistic design of the word "Muhammad" based on Arabic script (separate letters). It is the main component of the piece designed by Mr. Mandi, which reflects transparent harmony between the artistic designs of the word "MUHAMMAD" in Arabic and English scripts.

206

The Museum of Islamic Art, Qatar: *MIA Opened to the public in December 2008, designed by American architect I. M. Pei, the famous designer of the Louvre in Pyramid. The displayed artifacts in the museum reflect the plurality and diversity in the arts of the Islamic world.*

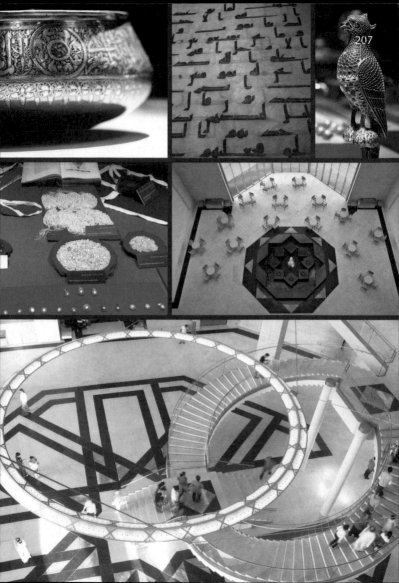

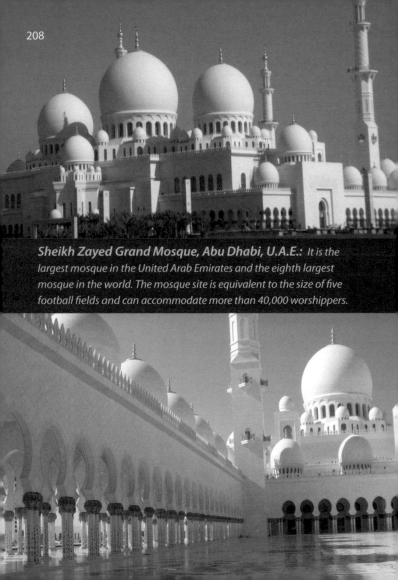

Sheikh Zayed Grand Mosque, Abu Dhabi, U.A.E.: It is the largest mosque in the United Arab Emirates and the eighth largest mosque in the world. The mosque site is equivalent to the size of five football fields and can accommodate more than 40,000 worshippers.

It has 82 domes and 4 minarets each 107 m high. The mosque has the world's largest carpet which measures 5627 square meters and the world's largest chandelier (15 m high and 10 m diameter). The mosque is considered as one of the most important tourist attractions in the U.A.E.

The Jumeirah Mosque, Dubai, U.A.E.: *One of the most attractive mosques in Dubai which reflects modern Islamic architecture.*

King Hussein Mosque, Amman, Jordan: *Was inaugurated in 2005 as one of the largest mosques in Amman that reflects the modern Islamic art and calligraphy. With its square shape and four minarets, it overlooks the city of Amman as it was built on a mount about 1000 me above sea level.*

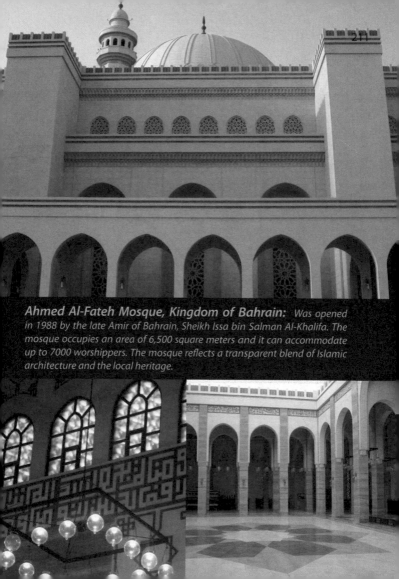

Ahmed Al-Fateh Mosque, Kingdom of Bahrain: Was opened in 1988 by the late Amir of Bahrain, Sheikh Issa bin Salman Al-Khalifa. The mosque occupies an area of 6,500 square meters and it can accommodate up to 7000 worshippers. The mosque reflects a transparent blend of Islamic architecture and the local heritage.

Al-Saleh Mosque, Sanaa – Yemen: It is the largest mosque in Yemen. It was opened in 2008, with an overall area of 224,000 m2 approx. and a capacity of 40,000 worshippers. The mosque was built in a Yemeni architectural style. It includes 15 wooden doors as well as 6 large minarets.

Sultan Qaboos Grand Mosque, Oman: *It is the largest mosque in Oman. It was opened in 2001 and includes the world's second largest hand-woven carpet and chandelier. (mosque area - 416,000 square meters, complex of the mosque extends to 40,000 square meters).*

Al-Aqsa Mosque, Jerusalem: *It is believed by Muslims that it is the second mosque placed on the earth for humanity to worship one God (the first one is the sacred mosque in Mecca). Al-Aqsa Mosque is a sacred place for Muslims and used to be the first **Qiblah** in Islam (the place Muslims used to direct their faces towards it when praying to God). After a Quranic revelation from God, Muslims were commanded to change the Qiblah towards the Mosque of Sanctuary in Mecca, which has the Ka'bah. The Al-Aqsa Mosque/ Sanctuary is about 14.4 hectare. It includes two important shrines, the "Qibli Mosque" and the "Dome of the Rock."*

Qibli Masjid

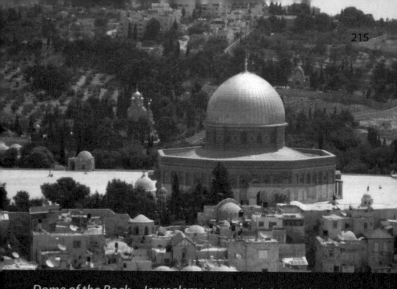

Dome of the Rock – Jerusalem: *It is an Islamic shrine and a mosque built in the period of 688-692 CE by the Umayyad Caliph Abdul-Malik Bin Marwan over the rock that is believed by Muslims the place where Prophet Muhammad ascended to the Heavens. It is an octagon building with a golden dome of 29.4m diameter.*

Umayyad Mosque, Damascus, Syria

*The Ummayad Mosque, established (706 -715 CE) under the Umayyad caliph Al Walid. It is one of the largest and oldest mosques in the world that has a great architectural importance (mosque interior is approx. 4000 square meters. The mosque holds a shrine which is believed to contain the head of St. John The Baptist (Prophet Yahya in Arabic), honored as a prophet by Muslims and Christians alike. **In 2001** Pope John Paul II visited the mosque, primarily to visit the relics of John The Baptist. It was the first time a pope paid a visit to a mosque. The minaret in the southeast corner is called the Minaret of Jesus as many Muslims believe that when Jesus returns, he will descend near this Minaret.*

The Great Mosque of Samarra, Iraq

A 9th-century mosque located in the Iraqi city of Samarra. The mosque was commissioned in 848 and completed in 851 by the Abbasid Caliph Al-Mutawakkil.

The Great Mosque of Samarra was at one time the largest mosque in the world; its minaret, the Malwiya Tower, is a vast spiraling cone (snail shaped) 52 meters high and 33 meters wide with a spiral ramp. The mosque had 17 aisles, and its walls were paneled with mosaics of dark blue glass. Minaret is in the style of Babylonian ziggurat.

Sultan Ahmet Mosque, Turkey: It is better known as the "Blue Mosque," with cascading domes and six slender minarets. Commissioned by Sultan Ahmet of the Ottoman Empire in the 17th century; construction began in 1609 and took seven years.

Ayasofya, Istanbul, Turkey
Aya Sofya (Hagia Sophia) in Istanbul is a former Byzantine church that has served as an Ottoman mosque for approximately 500 years. Now it is a major tourist attraction.

Taj Mahal, Agra, India : This is not a mosque, but a mausoleum built by Shah Jahan (1592–1666) in memory of his wife. Due to its unique architectural design, it is considered as one of the most important tourist attractions in the world.

▲ *Jama Masjid in New Delhi, India* The largest mosque in India, built in 1656

▼ *Red Fort, Agra, India*

▲ *Faisal Mosque, Islamabad, Pakistan* ▼ *Lahore Fort in Pakistan*

▲ Star Mosque, Dhaka, Bangladesh ▼ Auburn Gallipoli Mosque, Sydney, Australia

▲ Sultan Mosque, Singapore ▼ Sultan O. A. Saifuddin Mosque, Brunei

▲ Turkish Mosque in Tokyo, Japan   ▼ Mosque in Pattani, Thailand

▲ *The Crystal Mosque, Kuala Terengganu, Malaysia*
The mosque is mainly made of Crystal. It is located at Islamic Heritage Park on the island of Wan Man. It was officially opened in 2008

▼ Putrajaya Mosque, Malay

▲ *Kuantan Mosque, Malaysia*   ▼ *Mosque in Perak, Malaysia*

230

Al-Azhar Mosque, Cairo, Egypt: *Established in 971 CE , connected with one of the oldest operating universities in the world (opened 988 CE).*

The Ahmad Ibn Tulun Mosque, Cairo, Egypt: *Completed in 879 CE, one of the largest in the world, (26,318 sq m) it is also famed for its lovely architecture and unique minaret.*

The Mezquita of Cordoba, Spain: *Mezquita is the Spanish word for "Mosque." It is an 8th-century mosque designed by Muslim architects under the supervision of the Emir of Cordoba, Abdul-Rahman II (822-852). Today, the Mezquita is the Cathedral of Cordoba (officially the Cathedral of St. Mary of the Assumption).*

Alhambra Calat, Spain: Also called "the red fortress." It is a palace and fortress complex, constructed during the rule of the Muslim Sultan of Granada (1353-1391 CE). Today it is one of Spain's major tourist attractions exhibiting the most famous Islamic architecture in Spain.

Note: Within Alhambra, the Palace of Roman Emperor Charles V was erected in 1527 CE.

The Hassan II Mosque, Casablanca, Morocco: It was completed in
1993. Designed by French architect Michel Pinseau. The Great Mosque's minaret is
the tallest structure in Morocco and the tallest minaret in the world (210 meters).
At night, lasers shine a beam from the top of the minaret toward the Mosque of
Sanctuary in Mecca. (Capacity: 25,000 worshippers).

The Kairaouine Mosque, Fes, Morocco: *Founded in 987 CE. It is the second largest mosque in Morocco (after the new Hassan II Mosque in Casablanca) and one of the oldest universities in the world. Also, it is the oldest Islamic monument in Fes.*

▲ Kipchak Mosque, Ashgabat, Turkmenistan   ▼ Azadi Mosque, Ashgabat, Turkmenistan

▲ Shir Dor Madrasah, Samarkand, Uzbekistan ▼ Mosque in Bukhara, Uzbekistan

The Grand Mosque of Paris, France: *It is the largest mosque in France. It was founded after World War I and inaugurated on July 15, 1926.*

Note: In Islam there are five daily prayers. The following is a translation of the words of the "Azaan" (call for each prayer). Each statement is repeated twice: Allah is the Greatest. I bear witness that there is no deity but Allah. I bear witness that Muhammad is the Messenger of Allah. Come to the prayer. Come to the real success. Allah is the Greatest. There is no deity but Allah.

Mosque in Penzberg, Germany: The minaret is engraved with words of the "Azaan" the Muslim call for the daily prayers. The Arabic calligraphic design was made by acclaimed calligrapher Mohammed Mandi from U.A.E.

The Great Mosque of Xi'an, China

▲ Grand Mosque in Indonesia   ▼ Hui Mosque in Ningxia, China

▲ *Great Mosque, Touba, Senegal* ▼ *Mosque Faisal, Conakry, Guinea*

▲ Mosque in Bobo Dioulasso, Burkina Faso ▼ Djenné Mosque in Mali

Djenné is home to the world's largest mud mosque. This is more impressive than it may sound: the building is huge, and manages to be elegant both up close and from a distance. Two times a year all the city's residents drop everything, cart mud up from the nearby Bani river, and together they re-pack the Mosque walls.

246

Bibliography

Qur'an translations:
The authors relied on several English translations of the Qur'an and consulted with the original Arabic in our quotations:

Asad, Muhammad. 2003. *The Message of the Qur'an. Translated and Explained*, 6 vols. The Book Foundation.

Arberrry, A. J. 1996. *The Koran Interpreted*. Touchstone.

Hammad, Ahmad Zaki. 2007. *The Gracious Qur'an: A Modern Phrased Interpretation in English*. Lucent Interpretations.

Pickthall, Marmaduke. 1993. *The Koran*. Random House.

Saheeh Int. 2004. *The Qur'an: English Meanings and Notes*. Abul-Qassim Publishing.

Sells, Michael. 1999. *Approaching the Qur'an: The Early Revelations*. White Cloud Press.

Ali, Sultan Sohaib N., Ali, et. al. 2007. *The Qur'an and Sayings of Prophet Muhammad: Selections Annotated & Explained*. Skylight Illuminations.

Hadith sources:
Quotations from hadith, or sayings, of Muhammad come from several standard collections of hadith and are identified by the name of the recognized collector, such as Bukhari, Tirmidhi, Muslim, et. al. These collections are easily accessible online at www.sunnah.com

Arabic language sources:

Abdul Ghani, M. Ilyas. 2003. *The History of Al-Medina Al-Munawwarah*. Rasheed Publishing.

Al-Maghluth, Sami. 2008. *The Historical Atlas for Prophet Muhammad Life*. Obeikan.

Al-Zayed, Samirah. 1995. *The Inclusive Book About Prophet Muhammad's Life*. The Scientific Press.

Bukhari, Mohammad Bin Ismael. 1997. *Saheeh Bukhari*. Dar Al Afkar.

English language sources:

Adair, John. 2010. *The Leadership of Muhammad*. Kogan Page.

Ahmad, Mumtaz. 1996. "Islam and Democracy: The Emerging Consensus." *Middle East Affairs Journal* 2, no. 4:29-38.

Akyol, Mustafa. 2011. *Islam without Extremes: A Muslim Case for Liberty*. W. W. Norton. Armstrong, Karen. 1992. *Muhammad: A Biography of the Prophet*. Harper Collins.

————. 2002. *Islam: A Short History*. Harper Collins.

————. 2007. *Muhammad: A Prophet for Our Time*. Harper Collins.

Carmichael, Joel. 1967. *The Shaping of the Arabs: A Study of Ethnic Identity*. Macmillan.

Feiler, Bruce. 2002. *Abraham: A Journey to the Heart of Three Faiths*. William Morrow.

Hart, Michael. 2000. *The 100: A Ranking of the Most Influential Persons in History*. Citadel.

Hodgson, Marshal G. S.1974. *The Venture of Islam*, 3 vols. University of Chicago Press.

Islam, Yusuf. 1995. *The Life of the Last Prophet*. Mountain of Light.

Khalidi, Tarif. 2009. *Images of Muhammad: Narratives of the Prophet in Islam Across the Centuries*. Doubleday.

————. 2001. *The Muslim Jesus: Sayings and Stories in Islamic Literature*. Harvard University Press.

Mirza, M. Yaqub. 2014. *Five Pillars of Prosperity: Essential of Faith-Based Wealth Building*. Ashland, OR: White Cloud Press.

Al-Mubarakpuri, Safi-ur-Rahman. 1996. *The Sealed Nectar: Biography of the Noble Prophet Muhammad*. Darussalam.

Al-Nawawi, Y.S. 2003. *Riyadh Al-Saliheen. Authentic Sayings of Prophet Muhammad*. Darussalam.

Parrinder, Geoffrey. 1996. *Mysticism in the World's Religions*. Oneworld.

Rahman, Fazlur. 1997. *Health and Medicine in the Islamic Tradition*. Kazi Publications.

Ramadan, Tariq. 2009. *In the Footsteps of the Prophet: Lessons from the Life of Muhammad*. Oxford University Press.

Safi, Omid. 2009. *Memories of Muhammad. Why the Prophet Matters*. HarperOne.

Al-Sallaabee, Ali Muhammad. 2008. *The Noble Life of the Prophet*. Darussalam.

Unal, Ali. 2006. *The Holy Qur'an With Annotated Interpretation in Modern English*. Tughra Books.

Watt, M. 1974. *Muhammad: Prophet and Statesman*. London: Oxford University Press.

Wolfe, Michael & Kronemer, Alex. 2002. *Muhammad: Legacy of a Prophet*. DVD. Unity Productions.

Yusuf, Hamza. 2003. *The Life of the Prophet Muhammad* (24 Audio CDs). Sandala Productions.